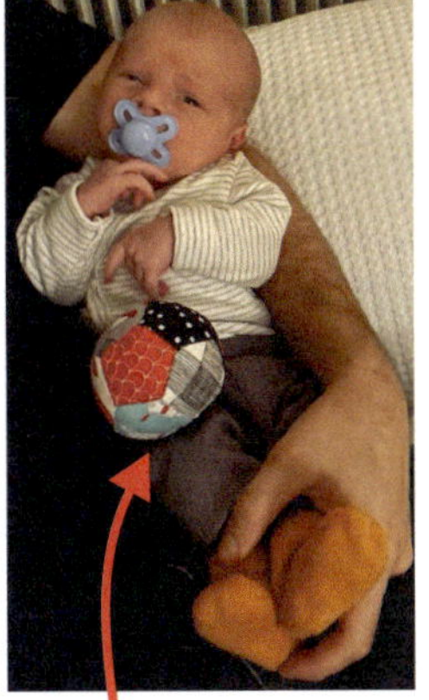

Even babies enjoy a dodecahedron!

They also like stellated dodecahedra!

Table of Contents

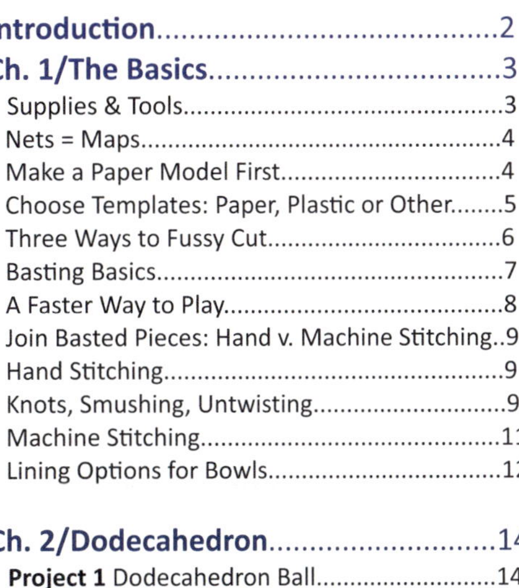

For Alan, who encourages this sort of behavior.

Profound thanks to Andrea Shlasko of Las Cruces, New Mexico, who as a result of the first edition of this book started teaching polyhedron-making, and generously shared her tips with me! The four polyhedra on the left (and more) are hers. To Helen Blumen of Bethesda, MD for her inspiring creativity and wisdom. Two of her unique pieces are on p. 2. To Mary Miller of Greenville, NC; her elegant, embroidered ball is on p. 17; and to Glenise Gallagher of Victoria, Australia, who made the cheery toys below!

Stitch-a-hedron: English Paper Pieced Polyhedron Gifts and Accessories to Sew

Second Printing, ©2023
1129 Stratford Avenue, South Pasadena, CA 91030
ISBN-13: 978-0-9799932-2-0

Questions? Comments? Did you make something inspired by this book?
I would love to hear from you and see photos!

cathy.perlmutter@gmail.com
Website: cathyperlmutter.com
Etsy Shop: https//www.etsy.com/shop/CathyPStudio
Instagram: @cathyperlmutter
Blog: http://www.gefiltequilt.com

Introduction: Very Brief Histories of Polyhedra, English Paper Piecing, & This Book

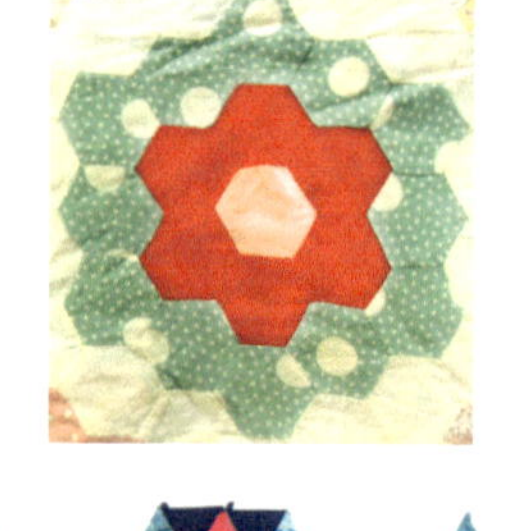

There are two kinds of projects in this book – closed "balls" and open "bowls". They can be hand or machine sewn. Their construction is rooted in two ancient fascinations.

One is English Paper Piecing (EPP), dating to 18th century England. Flat shapes (usually hexagons) were cut from paper. Fabric was wrapped around each piece. They were sewn together along their folded edges to create quilts. EPP had a revival in the 1930s and 40s, when the Grandmother's Flower Garden block on the upper right was made. EPP is now having another moment; people are using it to make dazzling, complex 2-D quilts. I wrote a book ("Hexagon Star Quilts," Landauer, 2020) about making them. One project from my book is in the photo on the right – quilters have gone way beyond simple hexagons!

Polyhedra – closed 3-D spheres made of shapes like squares, triangles, hexagons, etc – are a much older obsession. Ancient Scots, Muslims, Egyptians, Etruscans, Greeks and Chinese explored them. Plato discovered (or rediscovered) five, circa 400 BC, including the dodecahedron (Ch. 2). A century later, Archimedes worked out 13, including the truncated octahedron (Ch. 3), truncated cuboctahedron (Ch. 4), and icosidodecahedron (Ch. 6).

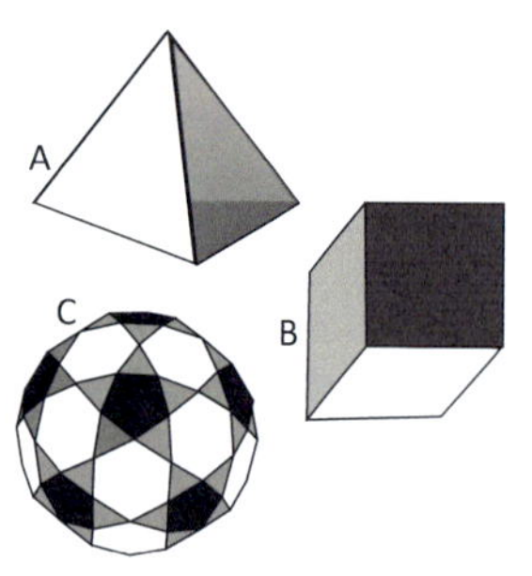

A polyhedron can be simple – like a tetrahedron, **A**, with four triangles; or a cube, **B**, with six squares. Or it can be complex, like a rectified truncated icosahedron, **C**, with 92 faces – 12 pentagons, 20 hexagons, and 60 triangles. There's an infinity of potential polyhedra!

They've fascinated me since my personal ancient history, high school circa 1972, when I made tricky stellated shapes out of balsa wood. These earned me my sole "A" in math. Years later, I became a quilter and bought Diane Gilleland's *All Points Patchwork* EPP book. One project was a dodecahedron, but I wanted something more ambitious. That led me to Gijs Korthals Altes website, 'Paper Models of Polyhedra' at https://www.polyhedra.net/en/. I used his nets (maps), and others on Wikipedia, to create my first fabric polyhedra.

Soon, I was stitching variations, and haven't stopped. Today is the best time in history to sew polyhedra. The quilting industry offers incredible colors and prints on sturdy cotton. There's also hilarious fabric, like the "Blah Blah" fabric that Andrea Shlasko picked for her cat ball, right (a bigger photo is on p. 29). Below it, I featured a wintry Cotton & Steel fat quarter pack, including a striking red cardinal, and a tiny skier on the square below it.

We now have technology that Plato (or whoever sewed his togas – Mrs. Plato?) never anticipated: Stiff fusible interfacing; glue sticks; and, of course, sewing machines. Fiber artist Helen Blumen machine-embroidered the hexagons in the "intention ball" on the right with adjectives like "curious," "creative," "friendly," "playful," and "flexible". For the ball below it, she printed wildflower photos on fabric. For baby gifts, Helen puts voice boxes inside colorful balls, and records a message or song. (Squeeze it and the message plays!)

Also modern is the compulsion to save the planet by upcycling the trash. This book includes projects made from coffee bags, chocolate wrappers, and more. Each was a challenge, some are scented, and they do keep a little refuse out of the landfill.

I hope you find yourself as excited about the possibilities as I am, and I can't wait to see what you do with them. Combining classical forms with new fabric (and sometimes old trash), to sew very personal toys and accessories, is rewarding, funny and fun!

Ch. 1/The Basics

Look through this chapter, but don't sweat the details. Then pick a project – the easiest are the dodecahedron projects in Ch. 2, or the truncated octahedrons in Ch. 3. As you follow the steps, you will be sent back to this chapter for specific instructions, and everything will make more sense!

Supplies & Tools

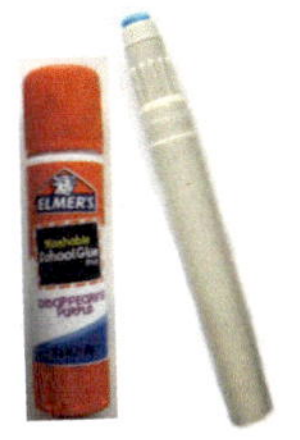

- **GLUE STICK** or **GLUE PEN** A washable school glue stick (near right), or a glue pen sold in fabric stores (far right). Any brand works, as long as the glue's not permanent. The pen's narrow tip reduces mess and improves aim, so it's especially useful if you bring these projects on the road, where you can't frequently wash hands.
- **CARDSTOCK PRINTER PAPER** Standard kind from office supply store. To print templates. See p. 5.

- **STRONG HAND SEWING THREAD** All-purpose, or quilting thread works; but if it knots spontaneously or shreds, try conditioner (below) – or different thread. Thin (80 wt) polyester threads like Superior's Bottom Line™, and WonderFil's DecoBob™, may shred less during hand-sewing, but are hard to see and feel, which can be annoying. Waxed two-ply 4-pound Silamide beading thread works well. All thread eventually shreds (especially when assembling bowls); cut short 12" pieces to minimize problems.

- **THREAD CONDITIONER** If your thread knots and shreds when hand sewing, try a conditioner. I use the beeswax kind in the photo on the right, with a slotted plastic casing to pull thread through. Other types and brands include "Sew Fine Thread Gloss™" and "Thread Magic™".

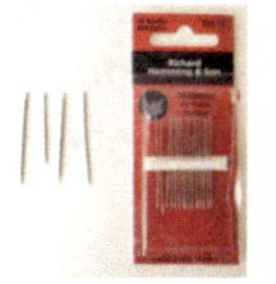

- **HAND SEWING NEEDLES** Slender, strong sewing needles are the easiest to use. I'm very fond of Hemmings size 11 milliners, but use whatever thin, medium-length needle that's handy!
- **STUFFING** Polyester stuffing for balls. (Not needed for bowls.) Brands include Poly-Fil™ and Fiber fill™.
- **STIFF FUSIBLE INTERFACING** or **KRAFT TEX™** or **CARDBOARD** For bowls (not needed for closed balls). Interfacing: I recommend Peltex™ Ultra Firm One-Sided Fusible Interfacing. (If all you have on hand is stiff interfacing with no fusible, or with fusible on both sides, those work too. Brands include Peltex™, Fast2fuse™, Timtex™, etc.) KRAFT TEX™ is very durable, but doesn't contain fusible. Plain cardboard can work for non-heirloom projects. See p. 5 for more information about these choices.

- **NONSTICK APPLIQUÉ PRESS SHEET** or **PARCHMENT PAPER** For bowls; If you use interfacing with fusible, you need this to protect the iron and the ironing board.
- **SCISSORS** Sharp and smallish for fabric. Plus another pair for paper/cardstock.

Optional but Helpful

- **SEWING MACHINE** Maybe. See top of p. 9. But even machine-stitched projects may have to be hand sewn for the last few seams. Machine must be zigzag capable.

- **CLIPS** A handful of paper clips, metal binder clips (I use the 3/4" wide size), or plastic sewing clips.
- **BALL-TIP STYLUS** (right). Also called an "embossing stylus." This inexpensive pencil-sized tool does a great job scoring lines on paper models, breaking through glue on cardstock templates and prying them out, with minimal risk of poking through fabric. One end should be at least 1.5 to 2 cm. Mine is from the "Royal Brush Embossing Set;" and something similar is in the "Artminds Embossing Stylus Tool Set."
- **PAPER PUNCH** If you want to punch a hole in temporary cardstock templates to help get them out. Not necessary if you have the ball-tip stylus above, or a small crochet hook.

Nets = Maps

Mathematicians call the flat maps for making polyhedron models "nets". There can be many different-looking nets for the same polyhedron. I tried to make mine as logical as possible for stitchers, to minimize thread-cutting.

I also added numbers. These do **not** necessarily indicate stitching order – they help you keep your bearings. **If you recreate the net accurately, almost any stitching order works.** Common sense will tell you which piece to add next! The worst that can happen is that you'll have to tie a knot and start a new line of stitching a few extra times.

It's usually most efficient to start in a center; then add surrounding pieces. From there, try to stitch from closed areas toward open areas for as long as possible.

There are "small" and "large" nets for most polyhedra. The size is at the top.

Most small patterns are separated by a red dotted line into two units. The line indicates where to attach shapes to make a full net for large patterns. It can also mark areas that form bowls.

Where there's room, I added a few "extra" pieces, outlined in magenta, in case you lose a piece (they tend to fly off tables and vanish). To avoid confusing yourself, don't cut them out until and unless you need them!

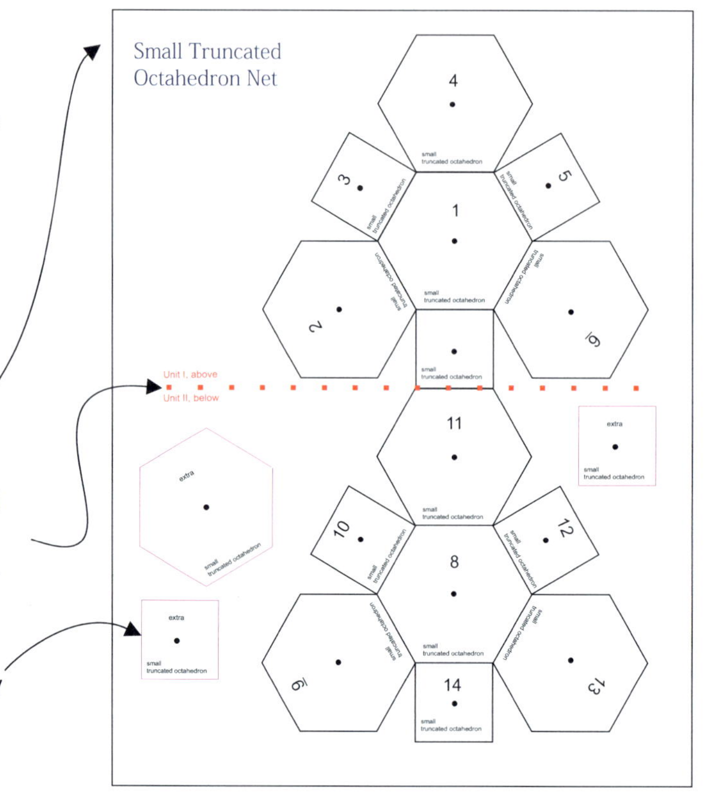

Make a Paper Model First

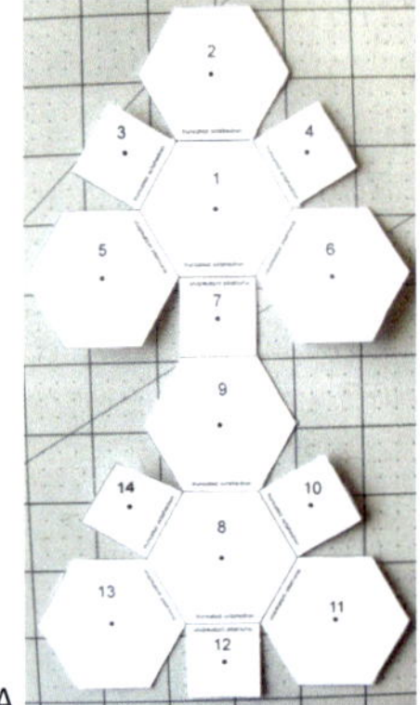
A

Whichever project you choose, making a simple paper model first is fast, fun, will deepen your understanding of the shape, and help you brainstorm creative options – from color placement to variations like flaps, lids, and windows.

It's easiest to use the small version of each shape for your model (because it's on one page). Print the net on paper or cardstock, cut out the overall shape, but **don't** cut apart the individual pieces, **A**.

Score the lines with a small ruler and pen, or a ball-tipped stylus, credit card, or anything that indents, **B**. A working ball-point pen is good for nets with lots of pieces, because you can see which lines you've already scored. "Scoring" means pressing firmly along the line, but **not** hard enough to cut the paper.

Gently fold pieces backwards along the scored lines, so the printing is on the outside. I use bits of painter's tape that won't rip paper (much) when removed. Write color or motif placement on chosen faces, **D**. Mark with a felt-tip marker or soft pencil so you don't have to press hard on the paper, **C**.

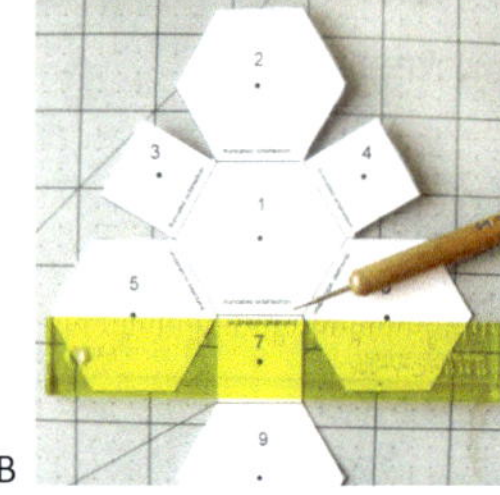
B

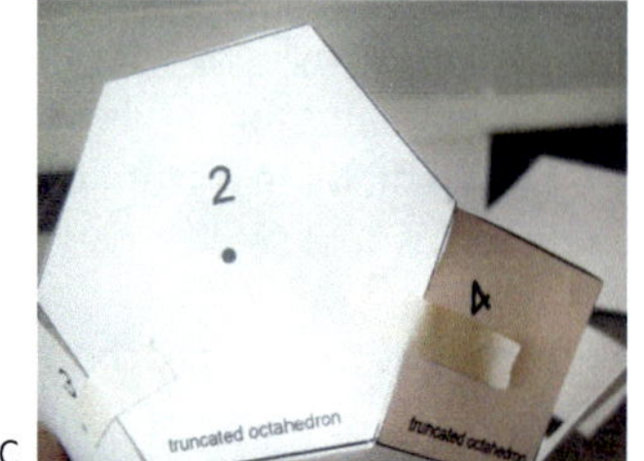

C

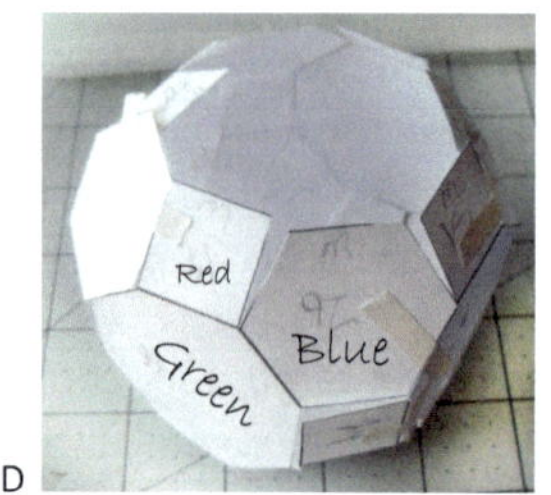

D

When it's time to lay out the fabric pieces, cut or peel off the tape, flatten the net again, and there's your annotated map! It tells you which color and shape piece goes where!

Choose Templates: Paper, Plastic, or Other

With traditional English Paper Piecing for quilts, fabric is wrapped around paper or cardstock shapes. In these projects, choices include paper, cardstock, stiff fusible interfacing – or something else!

Method 1

Cardstock Use as templates for balls. It will eventually be removed. Also can be used for some bowl linings. The standard kind from an office supply stores (65 lb.) works fine. Photocopy or print a net directly on it and cut out the shapes. Option: Punch a hole for easy removal. Don't punch out the central dot – you may need that to fussy cut (explained on p. 6, method 2).

If you don't have printer cardstock on hand, print the net on paper. Then cut pieces apart. Trace or glue each shape to any kind of cardstock (like a file folder), and cut out.

1

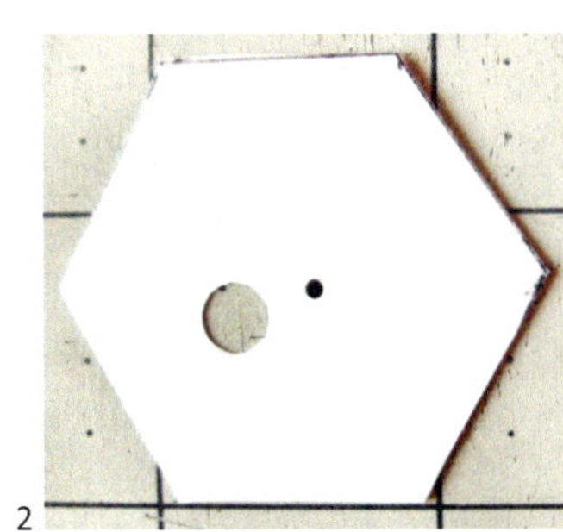

2

Method 2

Stiff Fusible Interfacing Goes under the featured side of most bowls. (Not needed for balls!) Several brands are in the supplies on p. 3. Interfacing without fusible works, but I prefer it with fusible on one side; it makes basting easier. Fusible on both sides works, too – but you must be extra careful not to smear it on ironing surfaces.

You will still print the net onto paper or cardstock first, as above. Then clip each shape to interfacing, and cut close around it (Don't pin; interfacing warps pins.) Or, draw a line around the paper or cardstock shape, onto the interfacing, then cut on the line; the marks will eventually be covered. Don't punch a hole in interfacing templates, because they will never be removed from the project.

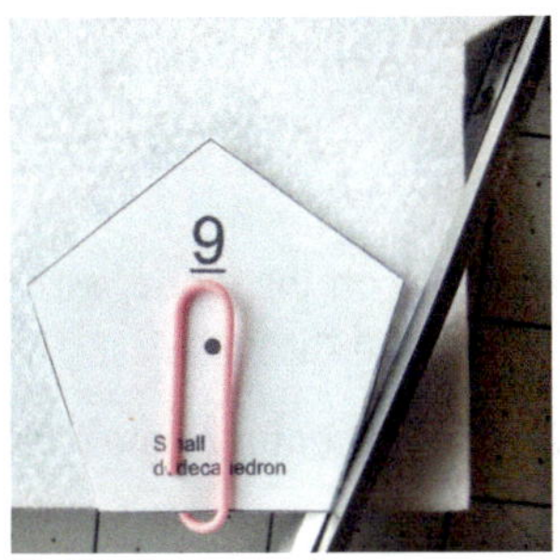

Method 3

Kraft Tex™ for bowls (not balls). It's a strong, leather-like, washable cardboard, used for handbags and mixed media art. It comes in different colors (grey here), and is even paintable! It can double as template **and** bowl backing, as in the bowl on the right, which only has two layers instead of three (The reverse side is denim from jeans).

Don't pin through Kraft Tex™ – holes are permanent. Use clips to trace around it and/or cut out the shape.

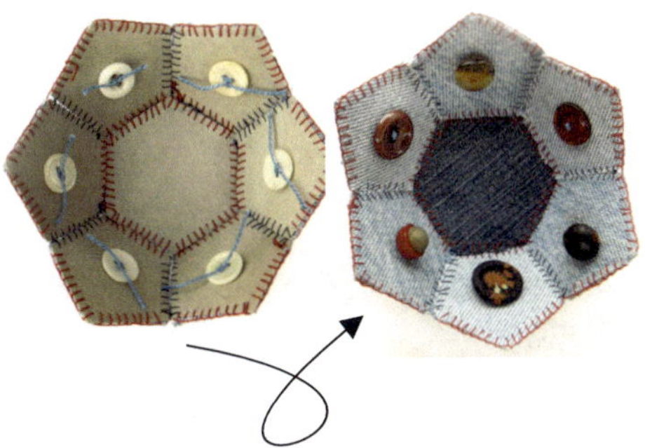

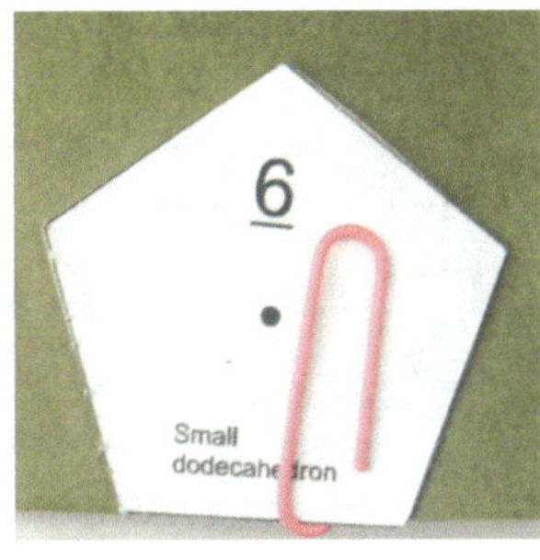

Method 4

Paper Use paper templates when machine-sewing a ball; or a bowl lining. Standard copy paper won't rip out stitches like cardstock can. Also use paper if your printer won't take cardstock, as described in method 1 above.

Method 5

Recyclables/Sturdy Cardboard Cardboard from cereal boxes, milk cartons, etc., can be used as permanent templates in bowls. They may not be as durable as interfacing or Kraft Tex™, but you're reducing landfill! If they have fun graphics, like the piece on the right, they can double as template and backing.

Three Ways to Fussy Cut

"Fussy cutting" means precise placement of printed motifs. It can create enchanting kaleidoscopic effects. In the bowl on the left, the rose was centered. Fabric for the four hexagons around it were cut in exactly the same place, so the stripes seem to flow in a circle.

Method 1

Make a Window

Print the net onto paper or cardstock.

A. Cut out a shape to serve as a viewing window. (If you start the cut with a rotary cutter, it will be neater.)

B. Use the window to scout locations on the fabric.

C. When you like the view, pin template back in the hole.

D. Lift away surrounding paper. Cut fabric 1/4"- 1/2" from the template all the way around. (Some people prefer 1/4"; some like 3/8"; I like 1/2". Try different seam allowances to find what you like best. With EPP, seam allowances do NOT have to be precise!)

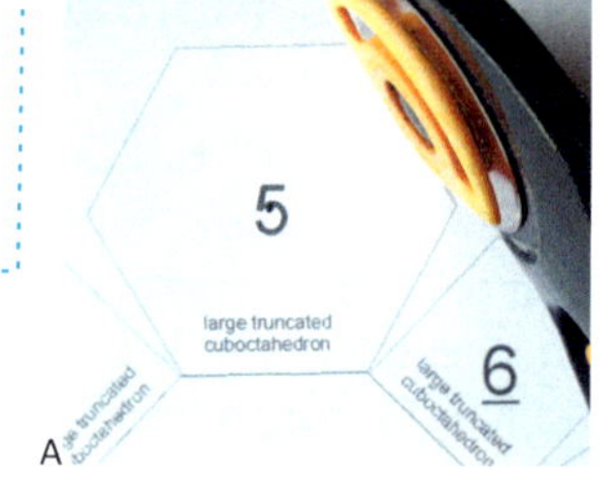

A

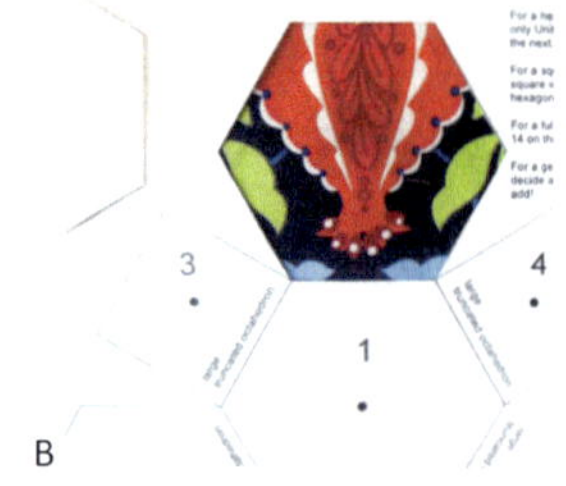

B

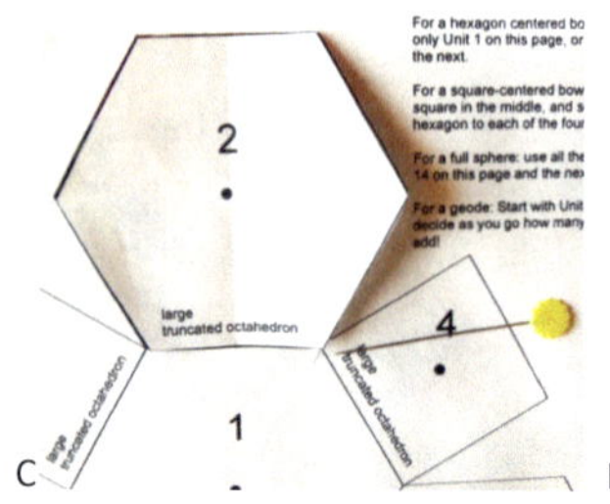

C

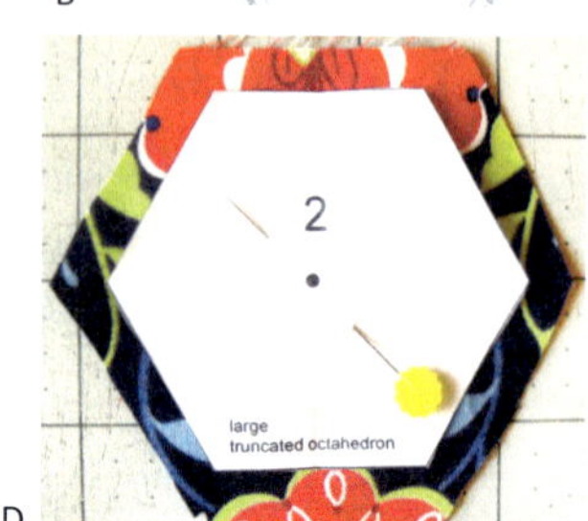

D

Method 2

Use the Center Dot

Here's how:

A. Place a cardstock template on the fabric, with the center dot facing up at you. Send a pin through it.

B. Push the pin tip through the center of the fabric motif.

C. Hold the paper or cardstock in position with a second pin. Cut out the fabric 1/4" -1/2" beyond the shape, all around.

You can also use this method to transfer a center dot that's on a paper or cardstock template, onto the interfacing. Mark the dot on the interfacing.

A

B

C

Method 3

Make a Plastic Template

A. Trace a paper template onto clear plastic (I like gridded plastic). Trace central dot with permanent marker.

B. Cut it out.

C, D. Find a location you like on the fabric. Trace the motif in pencil (which is erasable, so you can reuse the template.) Photo D shows the outline of the soccer ball in pencil, on the template.

E. Use the marked template to find the same configuration again.

F. Cut out as many fabric pieces as you need, 1/4"-1/2" bigger than the plastic template, all around.

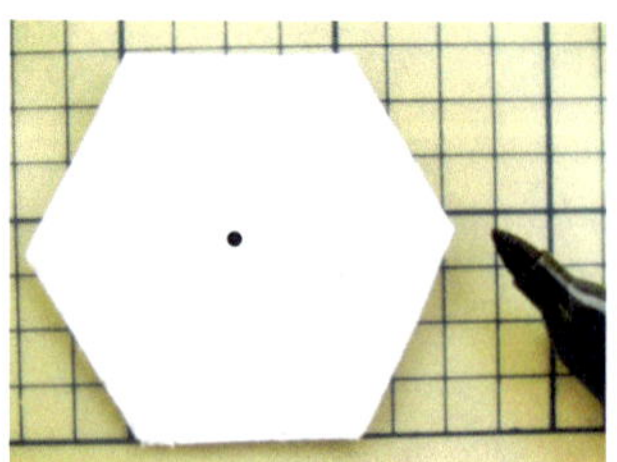

A

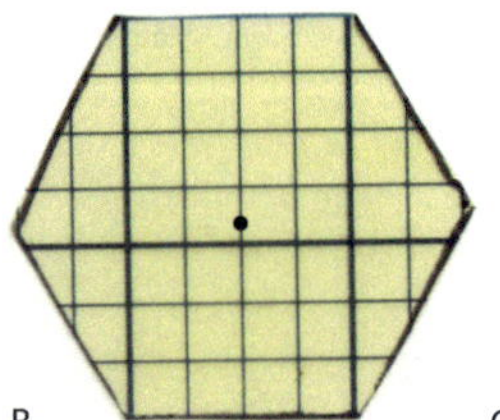

B

C

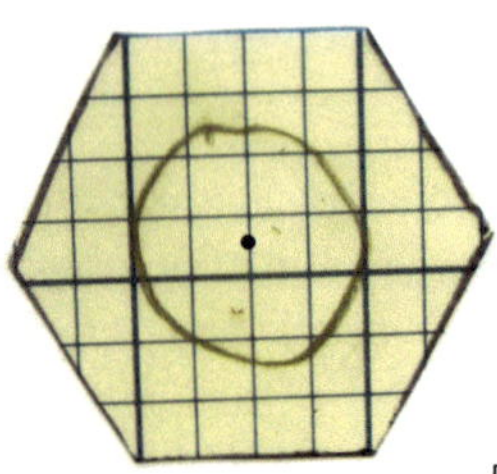

D

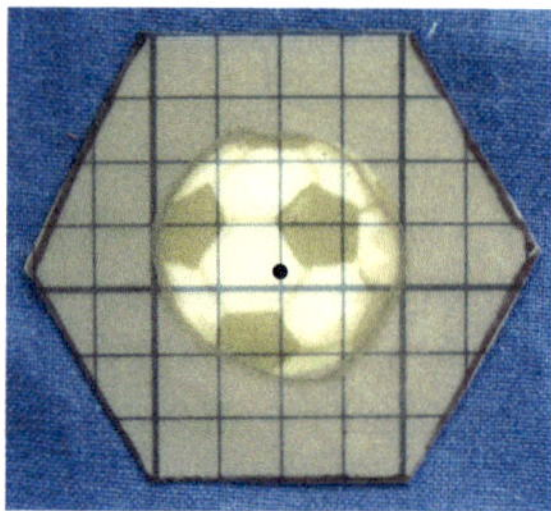

E

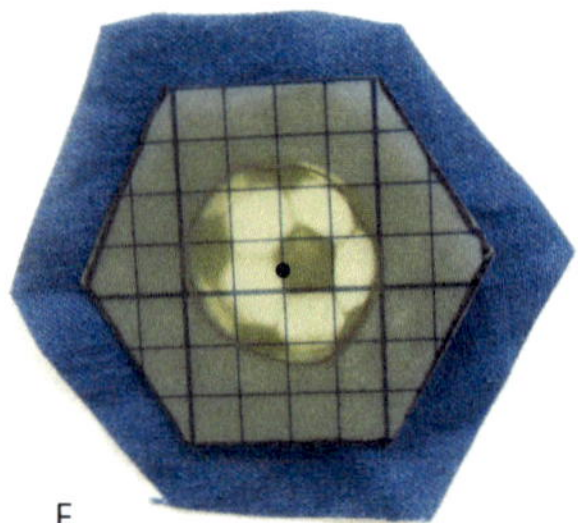

F

Basting Basics

When English Paper Piecers talk about "basting," they mean one specific step: Folding and securing fabric around a stiff template. Traditionally, the fabric is secured with long "basting" hand stitches. You *can* do that here. But today there are tools and techniques that make it faster, easier, sturdier and more accurate.

Method 1

Glue stick and iron, with paper, cardstock, or cardboard templates (If template is fusible interfacing, see method 3 on p. 8.) Place template on oversized fabric shape. Fold in each corner, glue and press. If template will be temporary (like paper and cardstock usually is), try not to get a lot of glue on it; focus on securing layers of fabric to each other. When a little glue gets on the template, don't worry about it, you'll ultimately break through it fairly easily.

A. Apply a little glue where you see the pink arrow, swiping the glue stick upwards.

B. Press the glued spot shut with a finger and/or iron, and dab a bit of glue on top if it.

C. Swipe glue above the next corner, moving left.

D. Press entire edge down.

E. Dab a bit of glue on top of that last folded-in corner.

F. Swipe more glue on the inside of the next corner.

G. Press the edge down. Repeat steps E-G for the next side.

H. Now you're at the second-to-last side. Swipe glue on top of the lower left corner.

I. Open the right lower flap and press the lower right edge up and behind it. Dab glue there.

J. All folded in. You earn an A+ if all the flaps angle in the same direction. Here, from the back, all corner flaps point clockwise. You could have made them all counterclockwise. Just be consistent with all pieces in the same project.

Basting Triangles?
A little trickier. My method is on p. 41.

Method 2

Iron, maybe with spray starch. Same as above, but with a lot less or no glue. I use this method to make turned-under linings on bowl pieces (lining method 3, p.13). Option: Lightly spray starch the fabric piece from its wrong side, especially if fabric is flimsy. Place template on back, printed side up. Press each edge inward as in steps A-J above.

I don't recommend this method for making balls – without glue, templates fall out too easily.

continued

Method 3

Fusible interfacing, ironing, a little glue With 1-sided fusible, the fusible should face up on the ironing board, to hold seam allowances in place. With double-sided fusible, the bumpier side (if there is one) should face up from the back. Use a press sheet to protect ironing surfaces.

Place template in the middle of the fabric piece. (If there's fusible on both sides, press the front first.) Flip to the back, and press each corner and edge inward carefully with the iron's tip. Follow the folding procedure in method 1, steps A-J on the previous page. You might need to use a glue stick inside some corners (right).

Method 4

Hand Stitching The traditional method. Same idea as method 1 – but with needle and thread. Works best with cardstock templates (Don't do it with fusible). It's portable, slow, and not as accurate as the methods above, especially with triangles. Don't sew through the templates, just the fabric layers.

Tie a knot at thread's end. Center cardstock template behind the fabric. Finger-press right fabric edge inward. Press top edge downward, **A**. At the corner, take a stitch through all fabric layers, and pull to the knot. Take one more stitch in the same spot – that's a tacking stitch.

Take a large stitch or two across the top of the shape, to reach the next corner. Again take two stitches in place, **B**. Continue like this, doing two stitches at each corner, **C**.

When you're back at the beginning, take three tiny stitches and cut the thread, **D**. Photo **E** shows a thread-basted hexagon.

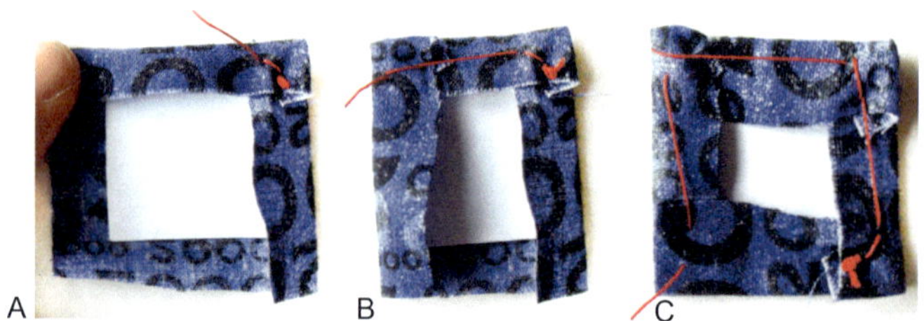
A B C

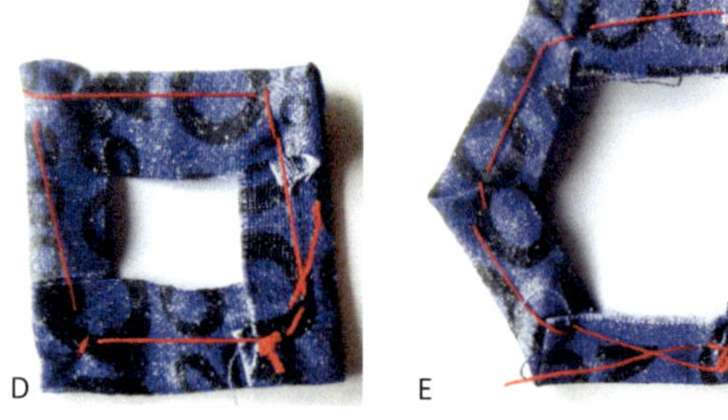
D E

A Faster Way to Play – No Basting Required!

Here's the fastest route to a finished bowl. Use stiff interfacing with fusible on both sides, if you have it. (If not, apply fusible web to the fabric that will cover the non-fusible side.)

1. Print a net onto paper or cardstock, and choose a bowl arrangement inside it, **A.** (The example is an icosidodecahedron, Ch. 6). Cut out an entire bowl shape. Don't cut the pieces apart!

2. Clip it to the interfacing. Trace around it.

3. Cut it out**, B**.

4. Fuse fabric to the front and back and trim away extra at edges, **C**. An appliqué press sheet or parchment paper will keep ironing surfaces clean.

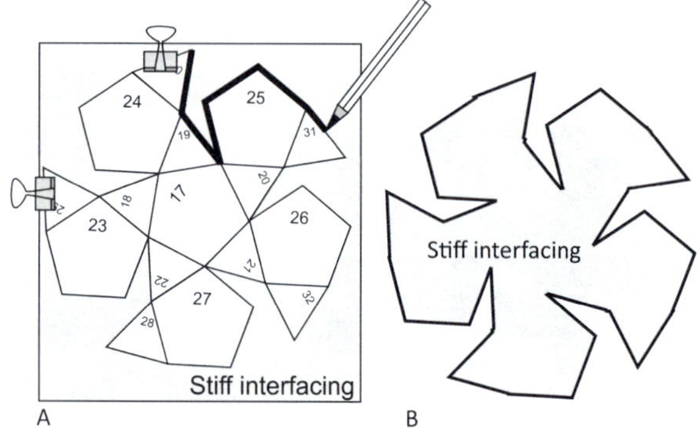

A B

5. Satin stitch each pair of circled edges together**, D**, using the machine stitching approach on p. 11. Then stitch all around the rim, **E.** Quick bowl! It's also a way to make jewelry – see the Soccer Flower Brooch on p. 57.

C

D

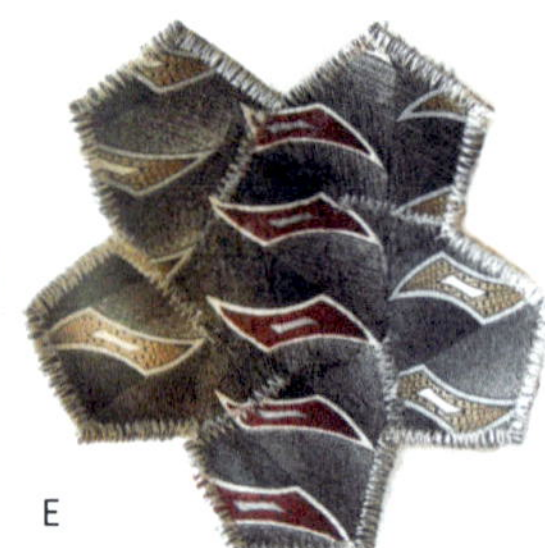
E

Join the Basted Pieces

Hand vs. Machine Stitching

Hand Stitching the basted pieces together is the slow, meditative route. Hand stitches show less than machine stitches. If thread spontaneously knots or shreds, try thread conditioner, or a different thread – see supplies, p. 3.

Machine Stitching with a zigzag, is **much** faster, and easier on hands. With invisible or matching thread, stitches are subtle, but still show more than hand stitches, because they're all on the surface. The more the shape curls up, the more challenging it becomes to machine-sew. For all polyhedrons and some bowls, even if you start by machine, the final seams still must be hand sewn. Machine sewing directions start on p. 11.

Handstitching Tips

What Knot?

BEGINNING: Any knot. Condition thread if it needs it (see supplies, p. 3). Make any substantial knot you like near the thread end. Take the first stitch from the back, or between layers. Pull thread so the knot rests against the fabric. Take two more tiny stitches in place to secure it.

ENDING: Loop knot Stitch a small loop, bring needle and thread through it twice, and pull tight (A). After the loop knot, do one of these:

- **IF THE BACK IS UNFINISHED:** Bring the needle and thread to the back and take 2-3 tiny stitches in the seam allowance. Do a loop knot, **A**, and cut thread.
- **IF BOTH SIDES ARE FINISHED,** or **WHEN WORKING FROM THE OUTSIDE:** After the ending loop knot, tie one single, tiny knot in the thread, a half-inch or so from where the thread exits the piece (circled in **B**). Bury the head of the needle back into the piece very close to where the thread exits. Travel it an inch or more away, **C**. Pull the needle and thread outward until the knot pops down between the layers. Cut thread close. Massage the end back between layers.

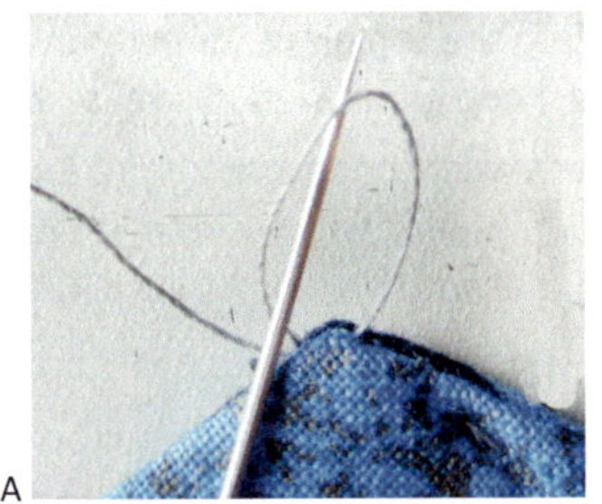
A

B

C

Smushing & Mushing, Pulling & Pushing

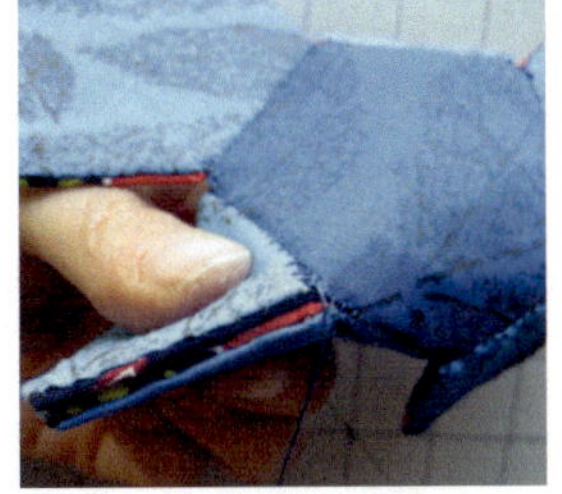

At the end of each edge, you often must move the templates into a different position, in order to stitch the next two sides together. This won't harm the project. If cardstock templates pop out, glue them back in, or remove and sew without them.

If corners don't match, push a bit on one side and pull on the other to align them. Use sewing or binder clip to hold pieces in place while you stitch.

Do the Untwist

Threads twist during hand-sewing. So every now and then, slide the needle up the thread, close to the project, where the thread exits the fabric. Hold the needle and project up in the air so only the thread dangles down. Stroke the thread downwards a couple of times, to work out the twists.

Hand Stitches

I use whatever hand stitch is easiest for the situation, and don't fret about using different stitches in the same project! Ladder stitch, and Andrea's whipstitch variation, are least visible; traditional whipstitch and lacing are often easiest. Try them all to discover which you like best!

Method 1

Whipstitch Traditional. Hold pieces good sides together, with edges to sew along the top, above. (Lefties: start on the left!) Pull knot between layers, or onto the corner's back.

Send needle tip away from you, through both seam allowances, *just* above the templates. Catch a few threads of each piece. Bring needle up in the air and back to the starting side. Repeat.

At the end of an edge, take two stitches in place and/or do a loop knot. Don't sew through temporary templates. It's okay to sew through linings as well as featured sides. Avoid sewing through interfacing; it's not necessary, and hard on hands. Whipstitching can show a lot, unless you do Andrea's variation, in the box at the bottom of this page.*

Method 2

Ladder Stitch One of the least visible.

1. Tie knot at thread end. (Lefties: start on the left.) Send needle into a corner fold, and out near the gap between layers, **A**. Pull thread to the knot, and sew two tiny stitches in place, **B**.

2. Dive into the lower piece, directly below where the thread exits above, **B**. Send needle tip left, inside the lower fold. Emerge. Send needle tip into the top piece, directly over where it exited the bottom piece. Keep aiming left. Travel a little more.

3. Emerge and go straight down into the lower fold. Continue across to the left. If you didn't tighten the thread, it would look like a ladder, **C**. Tightened, the stitches almost vanish, **D**.

A

B

C

D

Method 3

Lacing Stitch Works in many situations, shows more than ladder stitch. Great for working from the outside (photos 1-4); and for joining lined pieces to each other (far right photo).

1. Start with a knot under an edge or between layers. Bring needle out of the fabric. Take two tiny stitches in place.

2. Needle dives downward into the purple side. It exits just above the gap between pieces.

3. Needle dives upward into the pink side, and exits just below the gap.

4. Back down into the purple side, and out near the gap. Continue like this. Take an extra stitch at each corner. End with a loop knot.

Here the stitch joins two lined pieces' right sides together. You can catch only the featured sides; or linings AND featured sides if that's easier. Try not to sew through interfacing or other templates.

*** Andrea's whipstitch variation:** Andrea Shlasko teaches ball-makers this right-sides-together method for piecing balls (not for adding linings). The secret of its near-invisibility: Don't go through top edge folds. Enter and exit *just* below them.

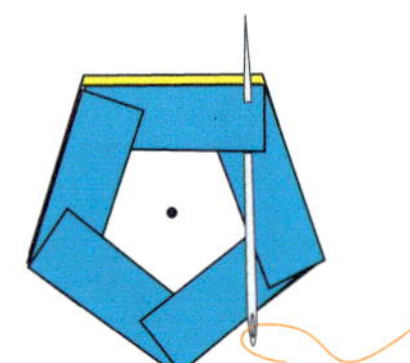
1. Pull knot between layers or under seam allowance. Don't go through the fold; push out needle just below it.

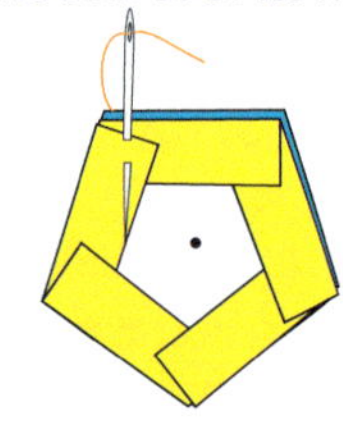
2. On the reverse side, insert needle downward, entering just below the fold.

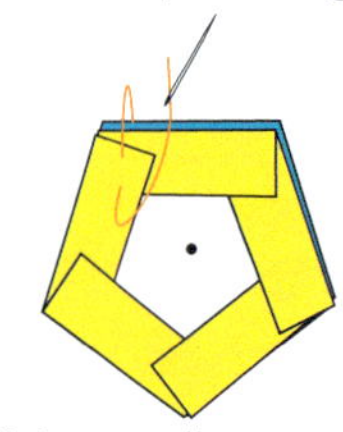
3. Bring needle up , around, and back to first side, **without** taking a stitch through either side.

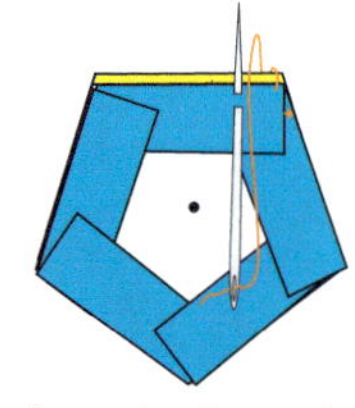
4. Back on the first side, again stitch upwards, go over, and down through side 2. Then return to side 1 without taking stitches. Continue like this.

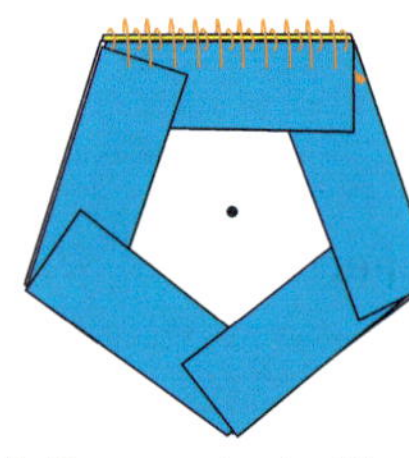
5. Do an extra tacking stitch or loop knot at the end of each side. A row of stitches looks like this.

Machine Stitching

Install an open-toe foot. Set machine to a very wide zigzag. Hide stitches with Invisible monofilament thread, or flaunt them with contrasting thread. Do a test run first to check tension, stitch width, etc., using samples of the same fabric, folded over scraps of same template material (cardstock, interfacing, paper) that's in your project.

Stitch the flat net first

A. When possible, start with a central piece (the blue pentagon, which will wind up surrounded by other pieces). Pull threads back, and do a few back-and-forth straight stitches next to the edge. Plant needle in the top corner of the blue piece. Bring a neighboring piece (pink) against it, with no overlap.

B. Switch to a short, wide zigzag stitch. Center seam under the foot. Press pieces together. Zigzag past 2, to the end at 3. If there are no more pieces to add there, do a few more back-and-forth straight stitches on the first piece, and cut thread.

C. But If there's another piece to add there, no need to do backstitching at 3. Instead, plant needle in the bottom corner of the first piece.

Lift presser foot and swivel pieces so the next edge lies straight in front of you. Bring up the next piece (green) and push it against the side of the first piece. Zigzag to the end, at 4. Again, if there are no more pieces to add there, do a few back- and-forth straight stitches on one side.

If you can add more pieces there, keep going this way! Eventually, you'll have to stop, do back and forth straight stitches, and cut threads. Then you may have to start again at a different location. Sewing the flat net this way is very easy.

Stitch into the third dimension

Now comes the challenge – stitching the seams that pull the piece into the third dimension. If possible, switch your machine to a freearm. Stitch with the bowl cupping up or down over the machine's arm, whichever you prefer.

D. Put the start of the seam under the foot. The corners closest to you, at "x" in diagram D – should NOT meet YET. The top corners of the green and pink pentagons (the "y'"s) are JUST touching. If not, pull them SLIGHTLY together.

On one side, at "y," take a couple of forward and back straight stitches (magenta in the diagram). Switch to a wide zigzag and center the seam under the foot. Do 1 to 2 zigzags in place. Then zigzag one stitch forward.

E. Take one more zigzag stitch or two, with the "y" edges getting closer.

F. Be prepared for action! Somewhere between your 2nd and 6th zigzag, the edges will demand to snap together! Help them along by bringing the "x" corners together. Stitch on, with edges pressed together firmly.

At the end, do a few back and forth straight stitches to secure the thread.

As a final step, you may want to add a decorative zigzag stitch around the rim, which can match or be different from the internal stitching.

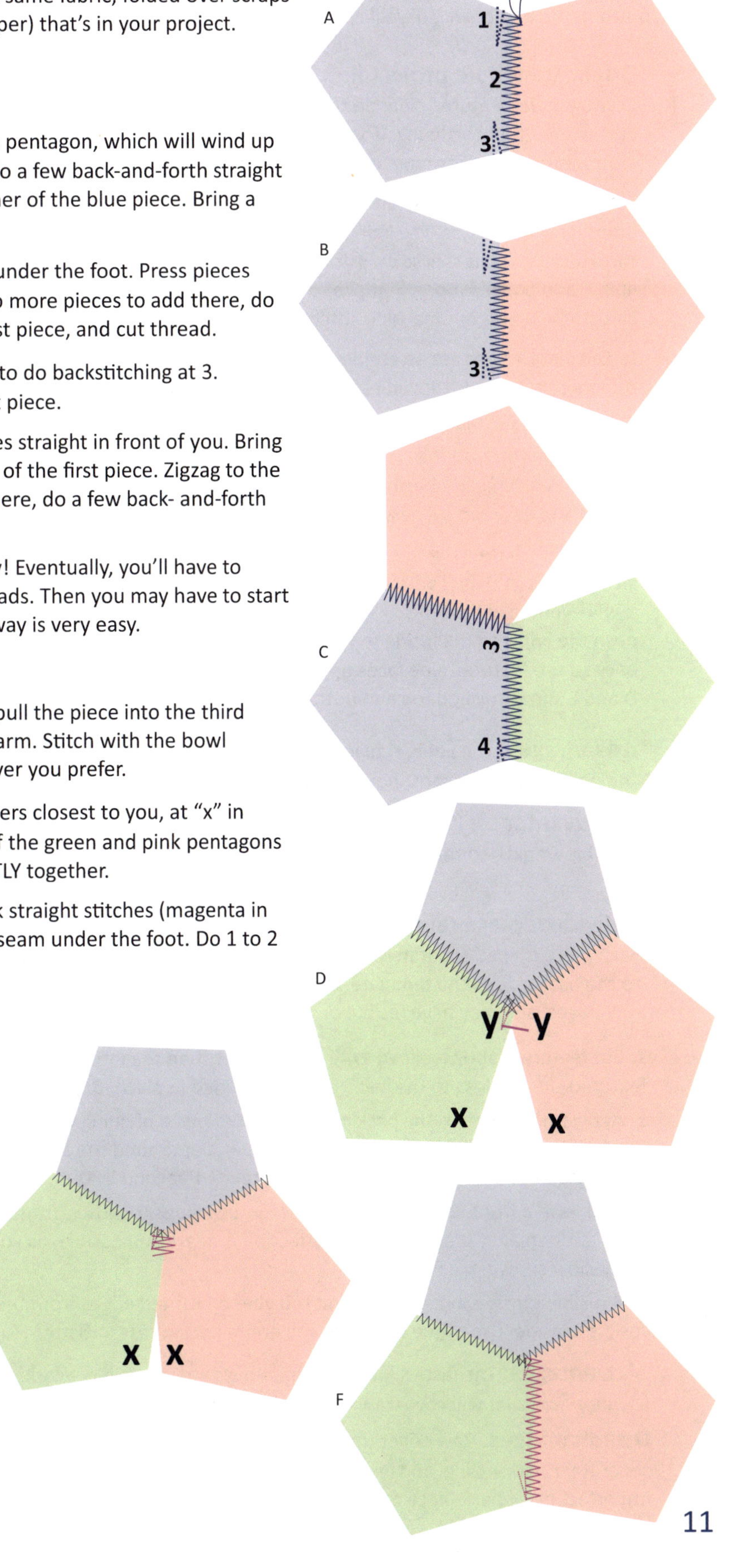

Lining Options for Bowls

With bowls, the inside is usually the most visible. So we'll call the inside the **featured side**. The less visible side is usually the outer/bottom side of a bowl. So we'll call that the **lining side**.

Duplicate whole project lining

Construct the featured side; do the same shape arrangement for the lining. (Except: If your bowl is asymmetric, the sides must be mirror images.)

The featured side, on the left in **A**, has permanent interfacing templates. The lining, right, had temporary cardstock templates. (Use cardstock for a hand-sewn lining, and paper for one that's machine-sewn, because cardstock can rip out machine stitches.)

A

A. Once both sides are assembled, remove all cardstock or paper templates from lining. (Interfacing stays forever.)

B. Slip featured side into lining, wrong sides together. Align shapes around the rim. Clips around the rim are helpful – each piece's beginning and end help you align seams and ease out fullness.

B

C

C. Hand-stitch rims together. Use a whipstitch, ladder or lacing stitch (p. 10). If you start sewing with lining outside, it will eventually tighten so much that you may have to push the lining to the inside to finish. Then you can flip it back so the featured side faces up from the bowl. Photos D and E show finished top and bottom.

D

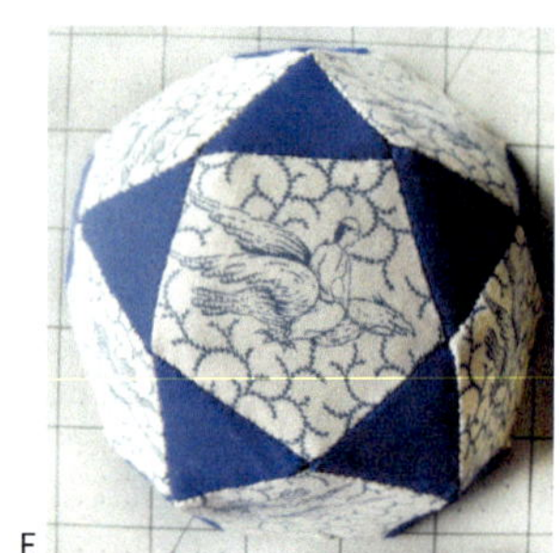
E

Advantages: The lining side looks great on the back of the bowl. This is the most polished-looking finish.

Disadvantages: If you flip the lining to inside, it might be a bit wrinkly, so these bowls may not be reversible.

Method 2

Individual piece raw edge lining

Each piece is lined separately. Featured side is cut **bigger** than the template and turned to the back side of the template. Lining side is cut the **same size** as the template, has raw edges, and may have fusible or glue holding it in place.

1. Cut featured fabric (yellow) 1/4" -1/2" **bigger** than the interfacing template, **A**. Wrap featured side's edges to the back, and fuse or glue in place, **B**. (See p. 8, method 3).

2. Apply fusible web to the back of an oversized piece of lining fabric (blue in **C**). Or skip the fusible and use lots of glue below in step 4. Cut around the template so lining is the **same** size as it, with **no** seam allowance extended beyond it, **D**.

3. You have a front, **B**, and lining, **E**. Place wrong sides together. Trim slivers off lining so it's slightly smaller than the front. Perfection is nearly impossible, as you can see from the yellow showing in **F**.

4. If fusible's inside, press lining, and rub glue on turned edges from the front. If no fusible's inside, use a glue stick over the entire back. Press to flatten, fuse, and dry glue.

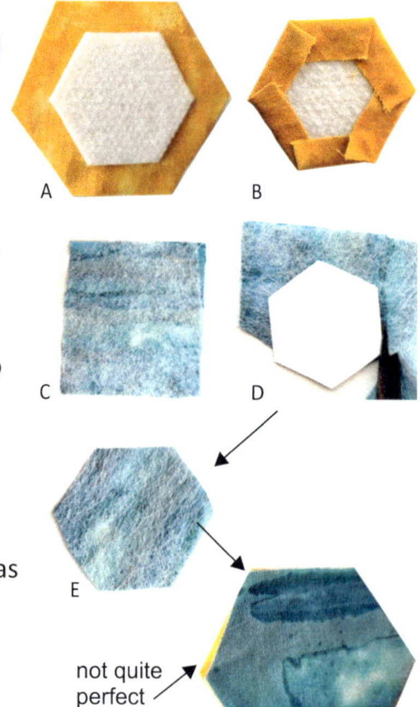

Advantages: The fastest lining option. Bowls are reversible. Works best if machine has a wide zigzag that will cover raw edges when panels are joined.

Disadvantages: Raw edges must be well-covered with stitches, or they can fray or separate. Hand sewing and imperfect machine zigzag may not cover all raw edges. Imperfect fit of back piece can look messy.

continued

Method 3 Individual piece turned-edge lining

A lining is stitched to each piece. The featured sides' edges (brown in these photos) go behind the stiff template; the (pink) lining is turned in on itself.

A. Print out templates. Use them to cut interfacing shapes. Baste featured fabric around interfacing. Bring edges to the back. Fuse/glue flaps in place.

B. Place one cut-out cardstock or paper template, printed side up, on the back of lining fabric. Cut out fabric 1/2" bigger.

C. Turn each side in around the template, following one of the procedures on pp. 7-8. Ironing method 2 on p. 7, with or without starch, works well here.

D. When starch and/or glue is dry, remove template and press again.

E, F. On back of featured piece, rub seam allowance tops with glue stick. Press lining pieces wrong side down, on backs.

G. Machine stitch finish: Load machine with thread that matches each side, or invisible monofilament. (Wind bobbins half-full of invisible; too much can explode them!) With lining side up, straight-stitch 1/8" from edges, all around. Begin and end with backstitches. Photo **H** shows a piece after sewing. Arrange pieces following the project's net, and join pieces by hand or machine.

Hand stitch finish: My favorite is a ladder stitch, p. 10 method 2. A lacing stitch can be easier, but shows more. No need to sew through interfacing; just through front and back flaps, wrong sides together. To bring this project on the road, see box below.

Advantages: Looks nice! No raw edges. Provides flexibility in designing a bowl – you can change panel placement as you go.

Disadvantages: Takes longer than the methods on p. 12, because lining edges must be turned. Not quite as neat as method 1.

A

B

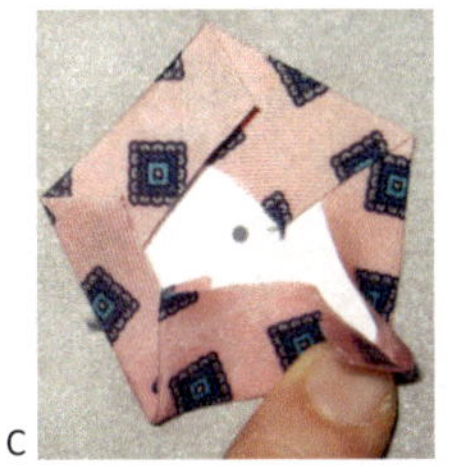
C

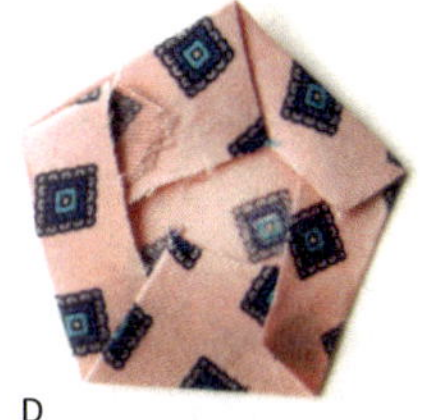
D

E

F

G

H

On-the-road hand-stitch lining: Try this instead of steps B-E above. It's like needle-turn appliqué; shape the lining and tuck in flaps as you go. Shown below with a triangle but it's easier with wider-angled shapes like hexagons, pentagons, etc. If featured sides contain fusible interfacing, prepare those pieces in advance.

1. At home: Featured (blue) sides are fused or glued around templates. On the road: Use those pieces to cut lining (pink) pieces, 1/2" larger.

2. Center featured side on lining, wrong sides together. *Triangles only: Cut seam allowances a scant 1/4" next to and above each corner. The rest can be 1/2".*

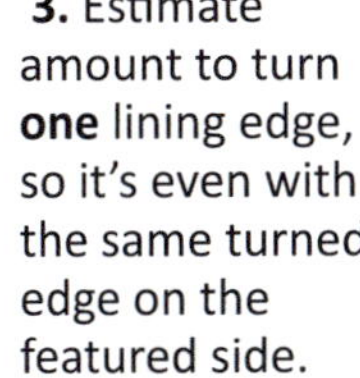

3. Estimate amount to turn **one** lining edge, so it's even with the same turned edge on the featured side.

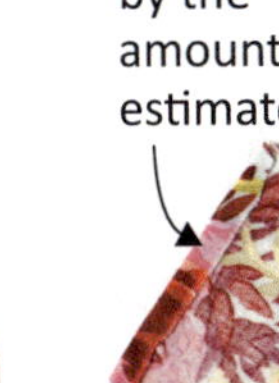

4. Finger press that edge inward, by the amount you estimated.

5. Use a clip to hold both turned edges together. *For triangles: Finger-press the next corner inward at an angle, so its fold is even with the tip of the featured side's corner.*

6. Finger-press 2nd lining edge inward, to match 2nd featured side's turned edge. Add clips to secure corner and edge.

7. *For triangles: Finger-press next corner inward as in step 5.* Turn in the next side.

8. All sides and corners are turned and clamped as needed.

9. Hand-sew lining in place. I first sent needle between layers from the right, so the knot was caught in the left pink seam allowance. Arrow points to emerging needle tip.

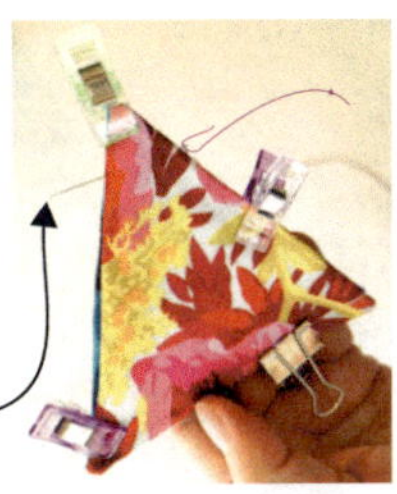

10. Needle travels down through blue fold to start the ladder stitch (p. 10). Continue around.

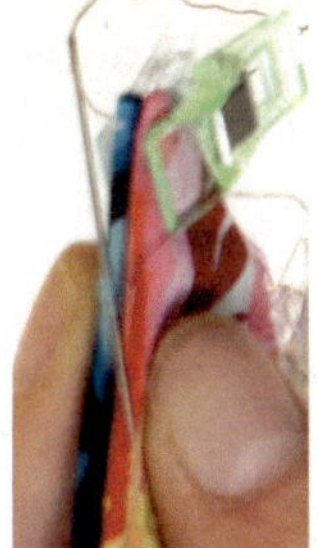

Move and remove clips as you go. At corners, I often switch to a stronger whipstitch, *especially for triangles.*

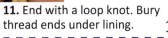

11. End with a loop knot. Bury thread ends under lining.

Ch. 2/Dodecahedron

This is a great place to begin an adventure in polyhedron-making! The bowls are very easy. So is the complete polyhedron, with 12 pentagon faces. Use fancy ingredients for a grownup gift, like the vintage silk neckties and mother-of-pearl button ball on the right. This could be a memory paper-weight. Or for a little one, use fun novelty fabrics! Put a bell, rattle, or voice recording box inside. Unique baby gift!

Left and above, two views of a necktie silk dodecahedron.

Project 1 = Dodecahedron Ball

Left and above, three panels of a baby ball. Every child should learn about Franklin Roosevelt!

Materials

– **Featured fabric** Small amounts of 12 different fabrics if you want each face to be different.

– **Cardstock or paper** For templates

– **Stuffing**

– **Embellishments** (optional)

See also supplies on p. 3

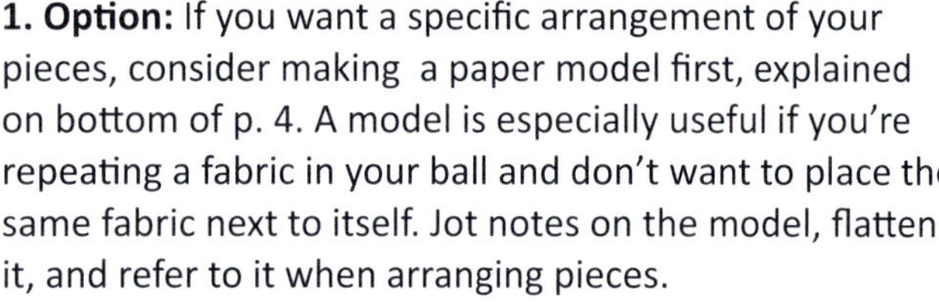

1. Option: If you want a specific arrangement of your pieces, consider making a paper model first, explained on bottom of p. 4. A model is especially useful if you're repeating a fabric in your ball and don't want to place the same fabric next to itself. Jot notes on the model, flatten it, and refer to it when arranging pieces.

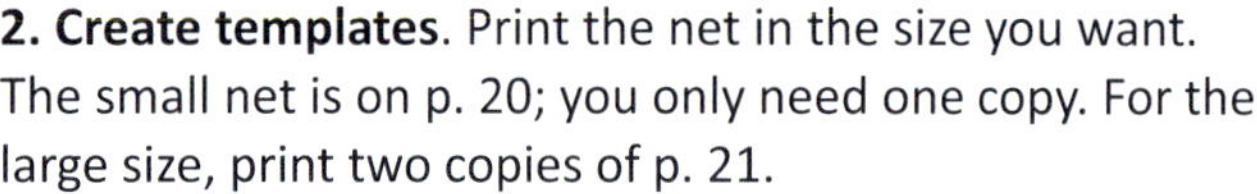

2. Create templates. Print the net in the size you want. The small net is on p. 20; you only need one copy. For the large size, print two copies of p. 21.

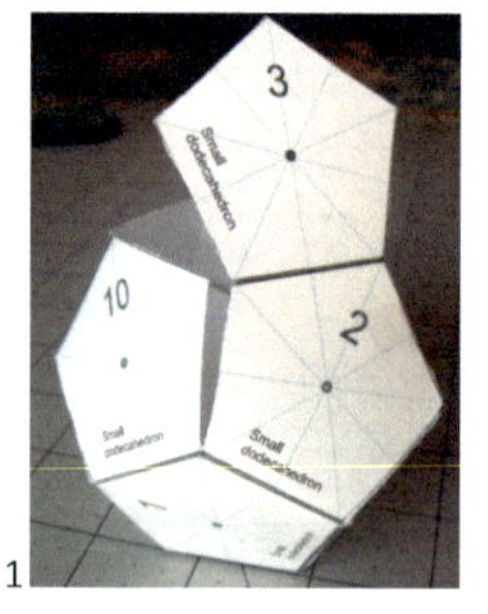

1

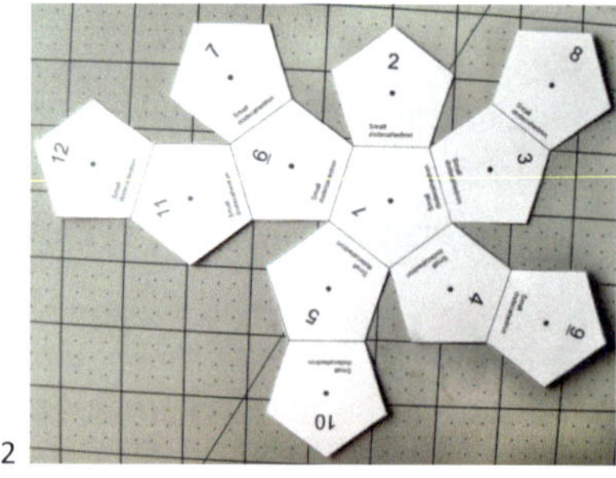

2

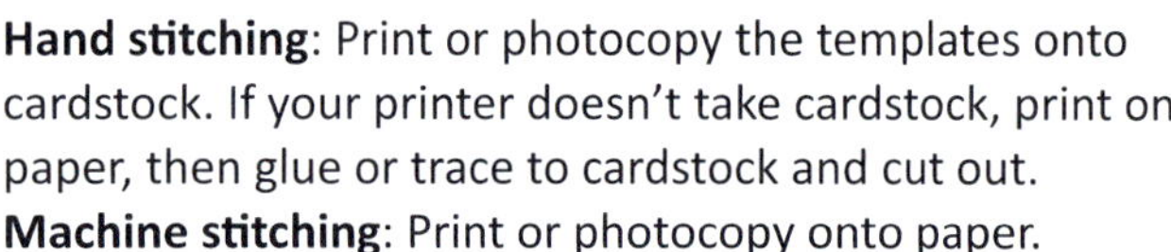

Hand stitching: Print or photocopy the templates onto cardstock. If your printer doesn't take cardstock, print on paper, then glue or trace to cardstock and cut out.
Machine stitching: Print or photocopy onto paper.

3. Cut apart the cardstock or paper shapes. Option: Punch a hole in each to make removal easier. Punch to one side, not the center, if you'll be fussy-cutting (method 2, p. 6).

3

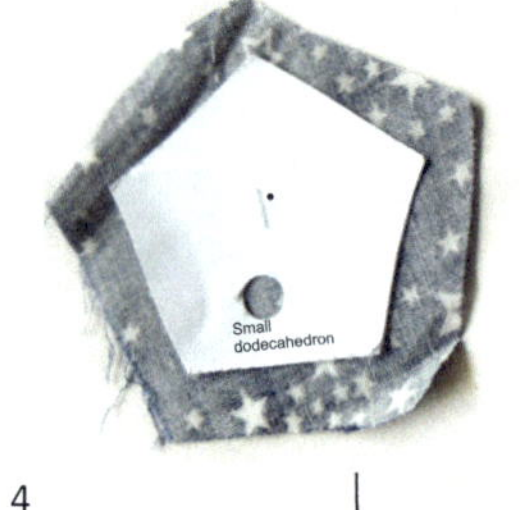

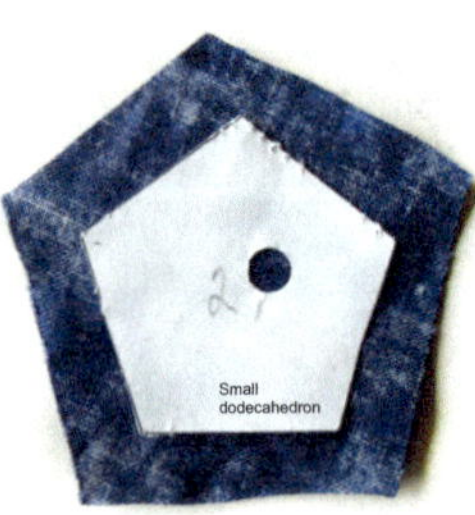

4

4. Place each template on fabric, and cut out the fabric 1/4"-1/2" bigger all the way around. (Some people like 3/8"! Try different seam allowances to figure out what you like best. They don't have to be perfectly consistent!) If you want to fussy-cut, see p. 6.

5. Wrap the fabric around each of the 12 templates. Photo 4 shows two pieces before basting, and photo 5 shows them afterward. Basting methods are explained on pp. 7-8. Here, I used a glue stick and iron. The printed side of the template should face up at you from the back.

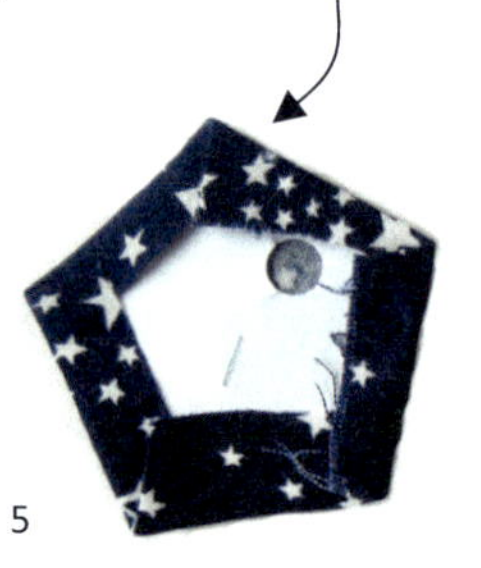

5

continued

6. Lay the 12 basted pieces out in the same formation as the net (and your paper model, if you made one.)

To minimize thread cutting, start stitching with the central piece (#1 on the net), and surround it with pieces 2-6. Keep going from there.

By machine: Follow the directions on p. 11, working from the right side.

By hand: Stitches you can use are on p. 10: a traditional whipstitch (or Andrea's less visible variation on bottom of that page); a ladder stitch; or a lacing stitch.

6

7, 8. Once you've recreated the flat net, sew the adjoining seams that curl the shape. Whenever possible, start from a closed area, and sew toward open areas. The numbering does not tell you what to sew next. Follow your instincts – it's hard to go wrong!

Machine stitchers will reach a point where the machine can't do it anymore – the shape has closed up too much. Then you must switch to hand-sewing. (See hand stitches on p. 10.)

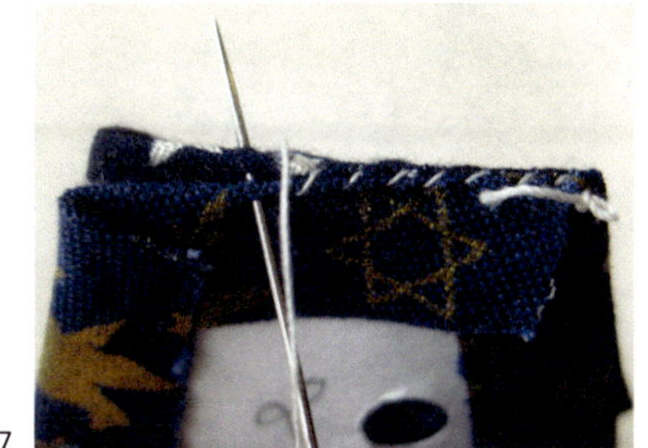
7

8

9. Keep stitching with wrong sides out until all but 2-4 edges are joined.

10. Remove templates. A ball-tip stylus can pry out edges and break through glue. If you punched holes in the template, use a stylus, chopstick, or crochet hook to pull them out through the holes.

9

10

11. Turn right side out and stuff. Use a pencil eraser or the wide end of a chopstick to push out dimpled corners.

12. Close the opening with hand stitches.

If you hand-sewed, your cardstock templates may be in good enough shape to use again! (You may want to iron them first!)

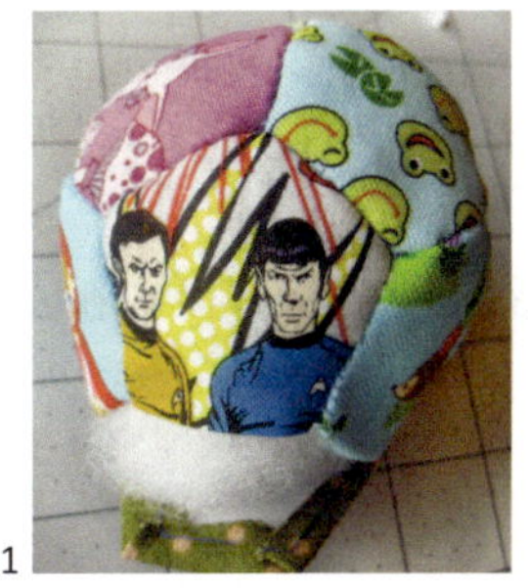
11

12

Project 2 = Half Dodecahedron Thimble & Bead Bowl

These bowls are easy, stack beautifully (left), and are especially good for holding beads – squish the sides to pour neatly. Or it can hold your thimble. For an elegant touch, I used necktie silks above. These can be hand or machine stitched.

Materials

– **Featured and lining fabric** Small amounts of up to 12 different fabrics if you want each face to be different, front and back

– **Cardstock**

– **Stiff fusible interfacing** See p. 5

See also supplies on p. 3

1. Print the small or large dodecahedron net onto cardstock. (Nets are on pp. 20-21.)

2. Cut out one cardstock pentagon. Clip it to stiff fusible interfacing, and cut out 6 interfacing pentagons.

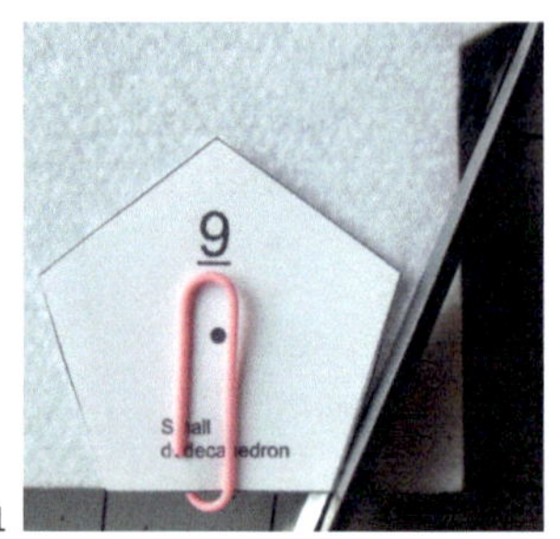

1

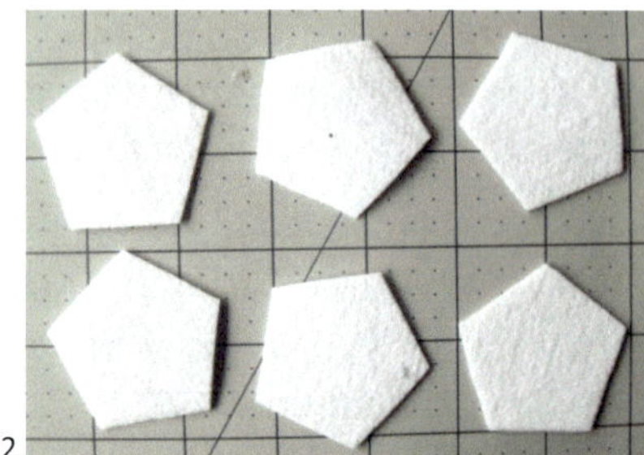
2

3. Use interfacing shapes to cut fabrics 1/4"- 1/2" larger. Place fabric wrong side up, and interfacing on top of that.

If fusible's on one interfacing side, that side should face up. With 2-sided fusible, if there's a bumpier side, that side should face up.

4. Baste featured fabric edges around the interfacing. Follow the procedure on p. 8, method 3.

After basting one side of all 6 pentagons, choose a lining method from those on pp. 12-13.

In this project, I used the individual piece turned-edges lining on p. 13. (Photos on that page show this same project). But you could do a duplicate whole project lining, or raw edge lining, p. 12.

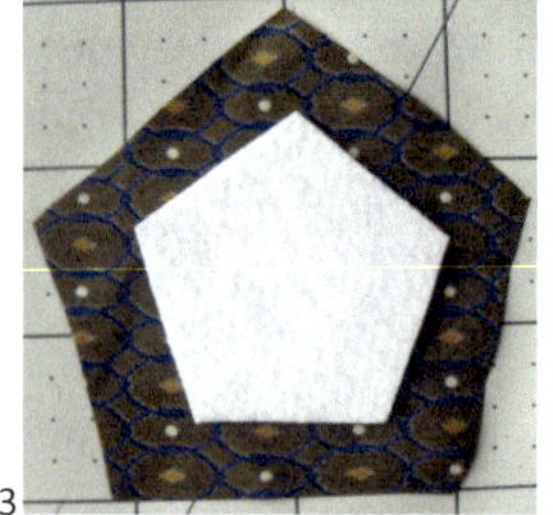
3

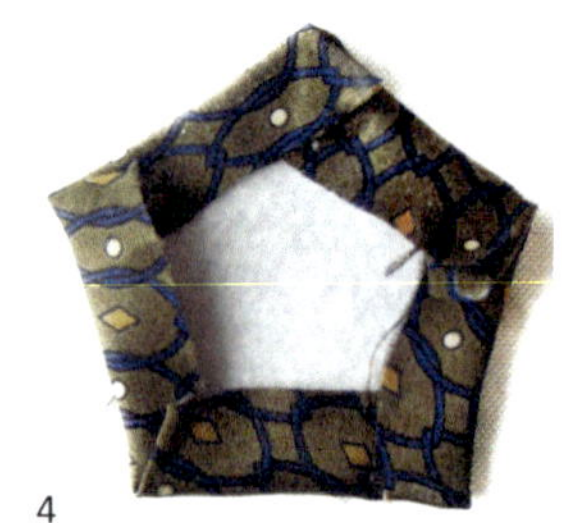
4

5, 6. Photo 5 shows a lining piece, all ready to be stitched to the back of a featured side with interfacing. Photo 6 shows it machine-stitched in position with a simple straight stitch. Or hand stitch it – a ladder stitch (p. 10) is usually the subtlest. Figure out what you like!

5

6

7. Arrange pieces as shown in the net and this photo, with a central piece (1 in the net), surrounded by pieces 2-6.

Hand stitchers: Surround the central piece. See p. 10 for possible stitches.

Machine stitchers: Use a wide zigzag stitch. Decorative thread is an option. I loaded a gold metallic thread top and bottom. Surround the center piece. Guidelines for machine stitching are on p. 11.

continued

7

8. When you've joined all the pieces, you'll have this. Congratulations, you have made what mathematicians call a "pentaflake"!

9. Photo shows the reverse side. (You can turn your pentaflake into a brooch – see box below.)

10. Stitch the five seams between the 'petals,' from the center outward, to pull the shape into a bowl. Start and end with a few tiny back-and-forth straight stitches, and use a wide zigzag the entire length of the seam, as explained on p. 11.

11. Consider doing a similar zigzag stitch around the rim, for decoration. Done!

8 9

10 11 12

Bonus Projects

Pentaflake Brooch

If you pause after step 7 on the previous page, stitch some beads and buttons in the center, and add a pin finding on back, you can have a brooch like this! A similar project with detailed directions is on p. 57.

Mary's Embroidered Dodecahedron

Mary Miller of Greenville, NC, made this gorgeous hand-embroidered ornament, using pearl cotton and a herringbone stitch over the seams. I think it has a Victorian look!

Shady Bowl: 2/3 of a Dodecahedron

Here are three views of a partially covered bowl, made with 8 pentagons. I used silk dupioni and brocade inside, and embroidered Chinese silk outside. I made a whole-bowl lining (p. 12. method 1).

Excavate your polyhedron!

This is like pulling in your stomach to show off your abs, if you had 12 stomachs, all with washboard abs! Pulling in the center flattens that side, showing off angles better. If you could pull it in even deeper, to the center of the ball, and imagine the concave face broken into triangles, you would have something like what mathematicians call an "excavated" polyhedron.

Dodecahedron excavated with thread only.

I think excavation makes these balls more interesting. They sit better on flat surfaces. They may be easier for small children to grasp. And this is a way to make them usable as dice – it will be clearer which face is pointing up than a ball with its bellies hanging out!

Right and below: Necktie slk dodecahedron excavated with thread and buttons.

Use strong thread, like upholstery, button or beading thread. The longer the needle, the better, but don't use a thick one, because then the starting knot won't stay under the surface. Tie a knot at thread's end. Send the needle anywhere into the ball and out through the middle of any face. Tug the thread until the knot pops below the surface and gets really stuck in there.

Take a couple of tiny stitches in the center of that face. Then travel through the ball to at least two faces away. Pull the thread taut until the first face pulls inward a bit further than you want it. Take a small stitch in the center of the second face, then insert the needle and bring it out from the center of another face that's at least two faces away. Keep going until you've put a stitch in each side.

To finish, pull on the thread and take a few tiny stitches in the center of the last face. Tie a knot in the thread, and pull it into the center of the ball. Bring the needle out anywhere, clip the thread close and massage the end back inside.

Partially excavated truncated icosahedron (Ch. 7). Only the pentagons are excavated.

You can pull in all the sides, or just some of them. In the ball on the right, I only pulled in the centers of the pentagons, not the hexagons.

You can excavate and embellish at the same time. If this is a present for an adult, consider adding a bead or button to the center of each face as you go.

Excavated icosidodecahedron with prints that interest babies. (Ch. 6)

If it is a toy for a baby or pet, do NOT add beads or buttons, because they are choking hazards. It's a good idea to ask the parent to check periodically to make sure the thread hasn't broken. If it does break, they should pull out all the thread. Then their polyhedron will revert to unexcavated status. (Unless they give it back to you to reexcavate?!)

Project 3 = Recycla-Bowls

Materials

– Foil or plastic food wrappers
Enough to cover six pentagons, front and back

– Cardstock, cardboard, interfacing or Kraft Tex™

– Glue stick

See also supplies on p. 3

Eat your way to fresh art! Above, left and center, is the top and bottom of a bowl made from orange bag labels. The bowl on the right was made from a cellophane pasta bag. The bowl below features chocolate wrappers.

For my first recycla-bowl, I wrapped my trash, er, graphic material, around cardstock templates, which stayed inside permanently. It's adorable, but flimsy. A more durable choice is stiff cardboard, like from a milk carton. For the sturdiest possible template, which can be laundered, consider interfacing or Kraft Tex™. These choices are further explained on p. 5. But never iron plastic or foil wrappers!

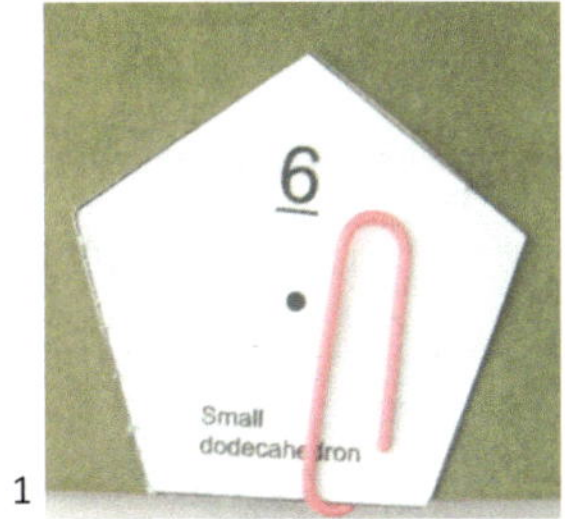

1

1. For lightweight permanent templates: Print a small or large dodecahedron net on cardstock and cut out six pieces.

For strong permanent templates: Print net on paper and cut out one pentagon. Clip it to the strong material (cardboard, interfacing, Kraft-Tex™, etc.). Cut out six pieces, as in photo 1 above (that's Kraft-Tex™)

2. Experiment with folding wrappers around the template so both sides are covered. If each wrapper ISN'T big enough to cover the back, see the box below.

2

3

3. If the wrapper is TOO big, you may need to trim back extra layers. Glue-stick everything lightly in position. Use clips to hold everything in place while glue dries.

4, 5. When glue is dry, stabilize each piece with machine stitching. I stitched from each corner to a corner two sides away, creating a 5-pointed star with gold thread, shown in photo 5.

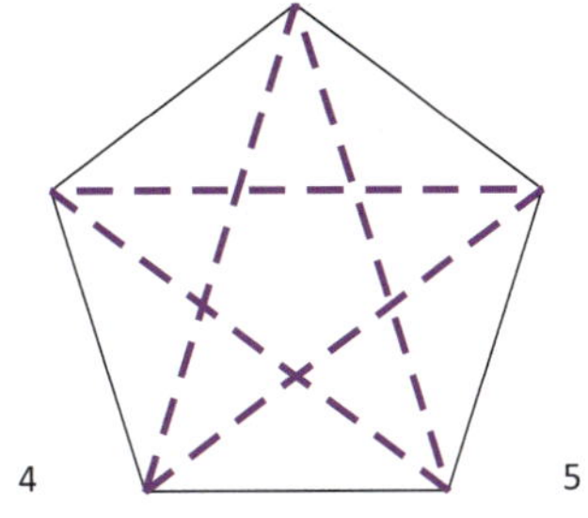
4

5

Tip: Start stitching in the same direction that the last flap on back is folded, so feed dogs don't push that flap out of position.

6, 7. Join the pieces by hand or machine. You'll first create a pentaflake – a central pentagon surrounded by five more, in photo 6. (Want to turn this into a brooch? See bottom of p. 17.) Last, stitch the seams outward from the center to create the bowl shape, explained on top of p. 17.

6

7

Way to cover a backside!

If the wrapper doesn't cover the entire back, and you don't want the template to show on back, slip something else inside. Here I cut a red plastic bag into pieces the same size and shape as the template. I lightly glued it to the back of the template, and then wrapped the featured side's coffee bag foil around to the back to cover the edges. Continue with step 4 above. It created a windowpane look for the back of the bowl on p. 51.

Small Dodecahedron Net

The full polyhedron: Requires 12 pentagons. If piece #1 is the base, #12 will be the roof. The finished ball will be about 3" across.

Basic bowl: Use only the pieces inside the red dotted line.

Stellated dodecahedron: This net corresponds in size to the small stellated dodecahedron templates on p. 70. Arrange those points on top of these pentagons.

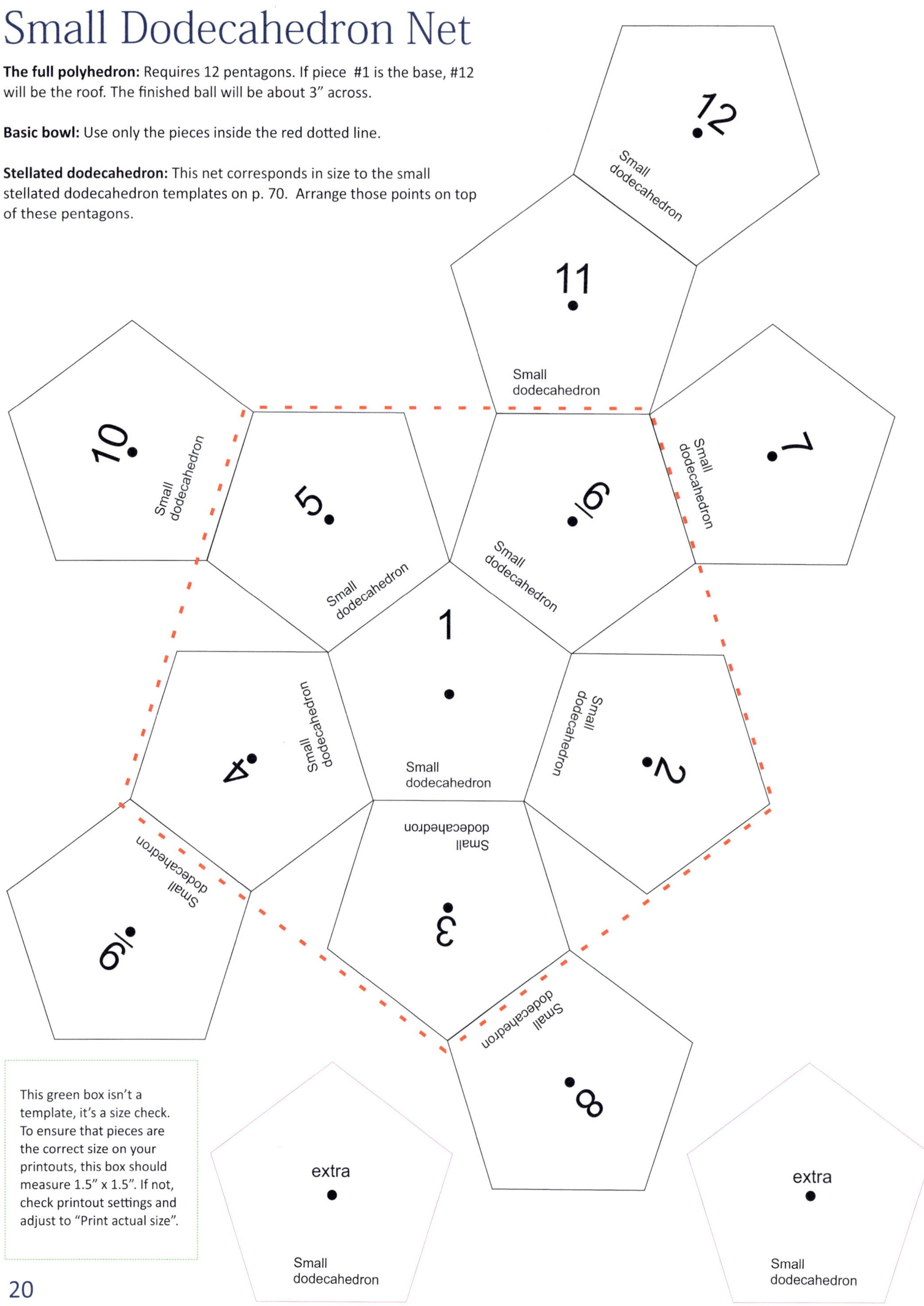

This green box isn't a template, it's a size check. To ensure that pieces are the correct size on your printouts, this box should measure 1.5" x 1.5". If not, check printout settings and adjust to "Print actual size".

Large Dodecahedron Net

The full polyhedron:
Requires 12 pentagons. Print out two copies of this page, and cut out pieces. Arrange following the small dodecahedron net on the previous page. The finished ball will be about 6" across.

Basic bowl: The numbered pieces on this page will create one bowl.

2.
Large dodecahedron

3.
Large dodecahedron

1.
Large dodecahedron

6.
Large dodecahedron

4.
Large dodecahedron

Large dodecahedron
5.

Stellated dodecahedron:
This net corresponds in size to the large stellated dodecahedron templates on p. 71. Arrange the points following the small net on p. 20; each represents one pentagon.

This green box isn't a template, it's a size check. To ensure that pieces are the correct size on your printouts, this box should measure 1.5" x 1.5". If not, check printout settings and adjust to "Print actual size".

extra
Large dodecahedron

Large dodecahedron
extra

Ch. 3/Truncated Octahedron

This easy polyhedron has just 14 sides. Eight are hexagons, and 6 are much smaller squares. As a bowl, it can rest on a hexagon or square base. Because it's simple, it's easy to make variations, like giving a bowl more or fewer sides. The bowl on top of this page is a planetarium, complete with spaceship (p. 26). The stuffed polyhedron directions start on p. 29.

Above, desktop planetarium, p. 26.
Left, Andrea Shlasko's "Blah Blah Cats" ball

Project 4 = Fancy Bowl or Beaded Geode

These directions are for a shallow bowl; or, for a more closed form that can become a geode, planetarium, purse – or whatever kind of vessel that you can imagine! I hand-stitched both projects, but you can use a machine most of the way if you prefer. The pomegranate bowl has 7 sides. The geode has 11; one is a flap. Although they look very different, the steps are nearly the same.

If you use the large-size templates (p. 31) the finished geode will measure about 5.5" in each direction. The bowl will be about 5.5" wide and 3" high.

Materials

– **Fabric** Small amounts for featured and lining sides. For the pomegranate bowl's featured side, I made sure there was enough of one print to fussy-cut 3 identical hexagons and 3 almost-identical squares. The geode's featured side below has 3 different purple prints; none are fussy cut.

– **Cardstock**

– **Fusible interfacing**

– **Beads, buttons** and/or other embellishments

See also supplies on p. 3

A

B

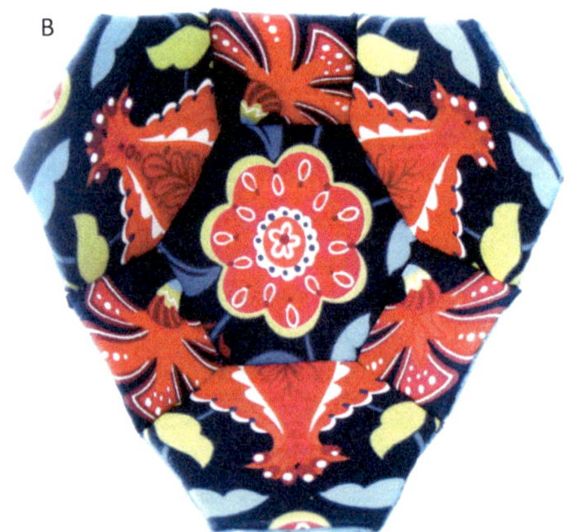

A - Pomegranate bowl, side view
B - Same bowl from above
C & D - Geode
E - Same geode with beading flipped to the outside.

E

C

D

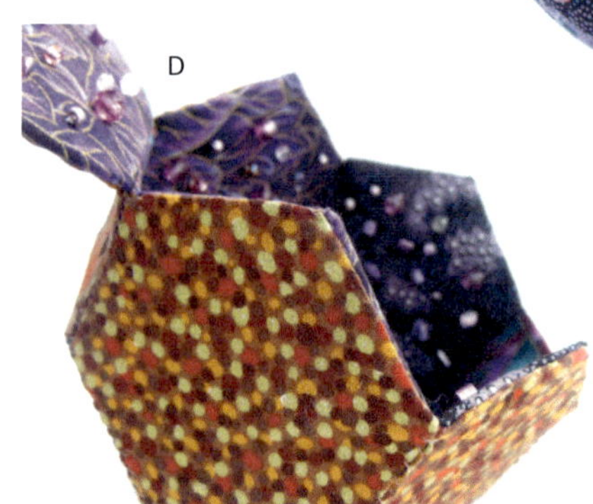

Fancy bowl or beaded geode, continued

1. Choose fabric. For my bowl, I used a gorgeous, large-scale print (designed by Alex Anderson for RJR Fabrics.) Each stylized pomegranate is about 3.5″ high.
For the geode, I chose three busy purple prints that evoked amethysts.
Consider making a paper model first to help you brainstorm fabric placement and creative options – see p. 4.

1

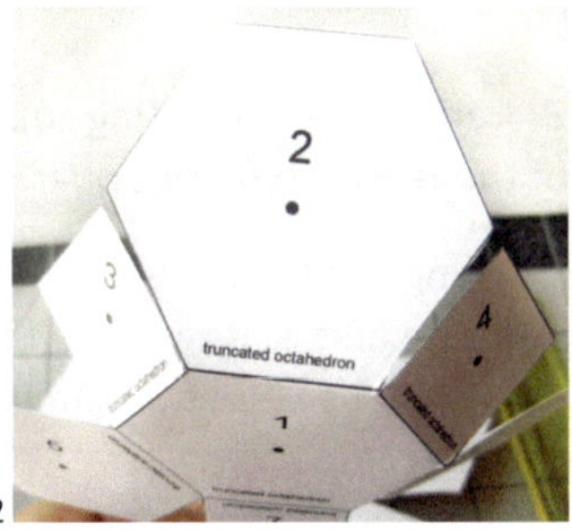

2

2. I used the large templates on p. 31 for both projects. Print the large net on paper (for now).

3. To fussy cut pieces like I did, read p. 6. Cutting a window from the paper printout will help you select locations.

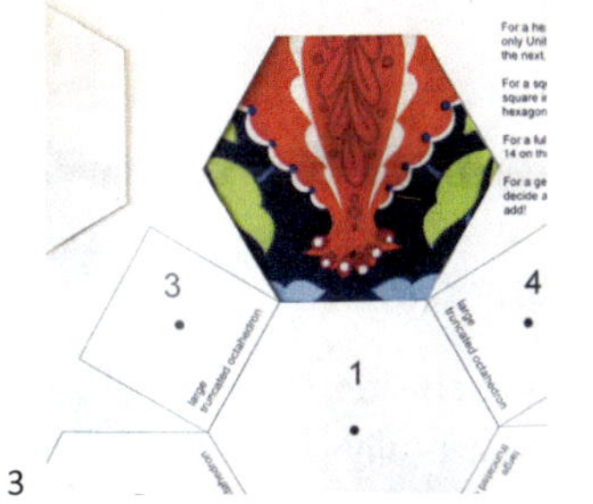

3

4

4. Once you like each location, pin the template there, remove the surrounding paper, and cut the fabric 1/4″ - 1/2″ larger than the template all around.

5. Use that first fabric hexagon to locate and cut out two more that have the same (or very similar) designs. Photo 5 shows the three hexagons I chose for each large side.

5

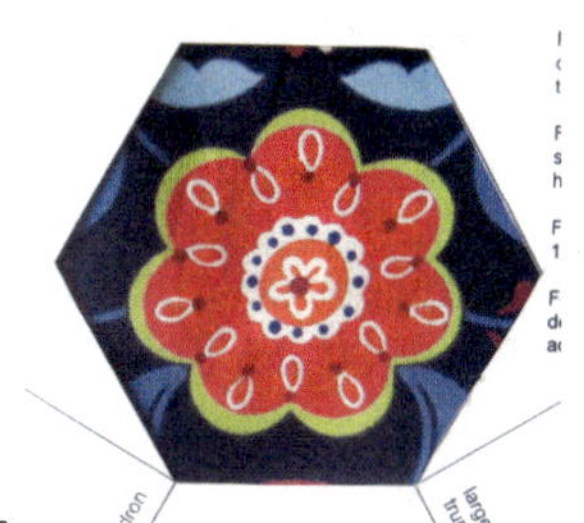
6

6. You need one more hexagon for the base. Repeat the same motif, or do something different – I used my window to locate and center a flower.

7. Here are the four hexagons required for my bowl – a flower base, and three partial pomegranate sides.

7

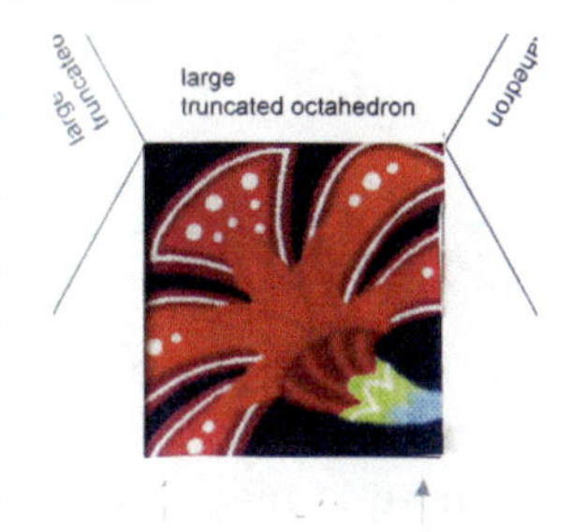

8

8, 9, 10. Use the square window to locate and cut three squares, 1/4″ - 1/2″ larger all around than the template. My square selections were similar to each other, but not quite identical. In photo 10 you can see that two of them were mirror images. (The third was identical to one of them.)

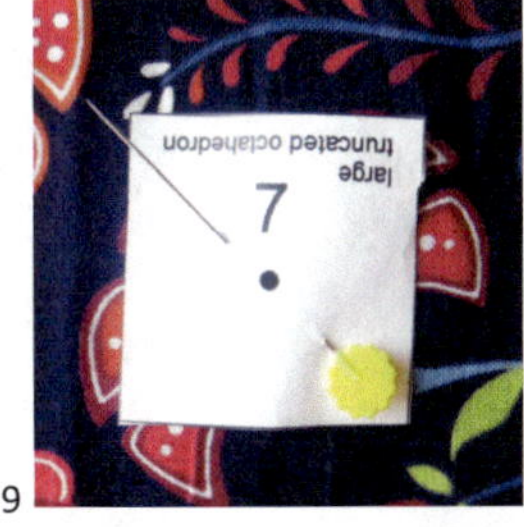

9

10

11. Use one of each template shape to cut all the pieces you need from stiff interfacing. Clip to hold the template in position while you cut. Or trace close around each shape and cut on the line. The markings will eventually be covered by fabric.

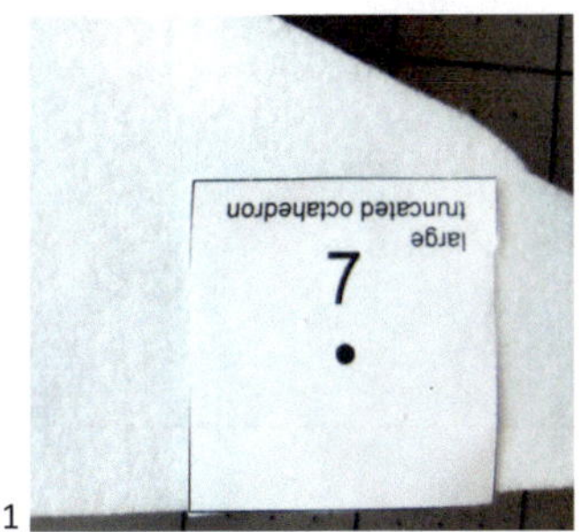

11

continued

12, 13. Center the interfacing squares on the wrong side of the featured fabric squares.

If interfacing has fusible on both sides: Press from featured side first, sandwiching the pieces inside a nonstick appliqué sheet or parchment paper on top and bottom.

If interfacing has only one fusible side: That side should be facing up at you.

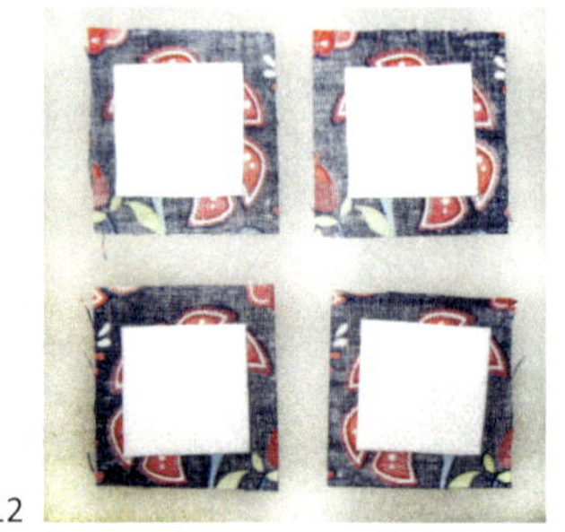
12

13

14. From the back, fold and fuse or glue each of the four fabric edges inward. Basting basics are on pp. 7- 8. Glue from a glue stick helps hold down corner layers.

15. Do the same for the hexagons, folding each side inwards, dabbing glue where needed, and carefully pressing in place.

14

15

If you're making a beaded geode (or anything else with 3-D embellishments), this is the best time to do it. Read 'Geode Interlude' below.

16. Arrange the pieces as you want them in the bowl, following the net on p. 30 or 31.

continued

16

Geode Interlude

Up through step 15 above, making a geode was the same as the bowl, except the former has more pieces. (I used 11 pieces in the geode, leaving out pieces #3, #4, and #5 from the net on p. 30.)

I stitched beads to the hexagons only (not squares), using strong beading thread. I added them after step 15, when one side of the interfacing had fabric, photo **A**. The beading thread shows on the back, **B**, but it's okay because it will soon be covered.

A

B

Do **not** attach beads within 1/4"- 3/8" of the edges. They would get in the way of stitching.

Continue with step 17 on the next page, to add lining, **C**, then join pieces. You'll probably have to do this by hand because heavily beaded pieces won't go safely through a machine. I added the brown-and-gold lining to each individual piece by hand, using a ladder stitch (p. 10), **D**.

C

D

17. Choose lining fabric for the bowl's back. I picked this blue print with light, medium, and dark areas.

Pick a method to line the bowl and a template type:

– I used the "individual piece turned edges lining," illustrated on p. 13. The "duplicate whole project lining" on p. 12 is also a nice finish.

– Use cardstock templates for easy basting UNLESS you will machine-sew a duplicate whole project lining. In the latter case, choose paper.

– Print templates on p. 31 onto cardstock if you haven't done so already. (Or, if necessary, paper.)

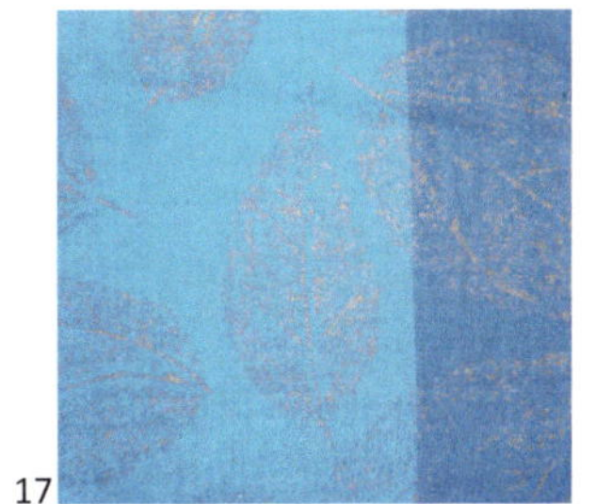
17

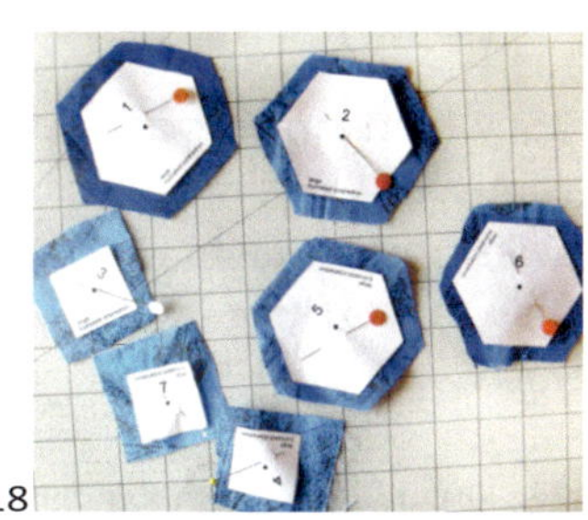
18

18. Cut apart paper or cardstock templates. Center each on the lining fabric, and cut fabric 1/4" - 1/2" bigger. If you want more than seven pieces, also print out Unit II on p. 32.

19. Use an iron and light glue, or spray starch, to fold edges around the template. Follow basting directions on pp. 7-8.

19

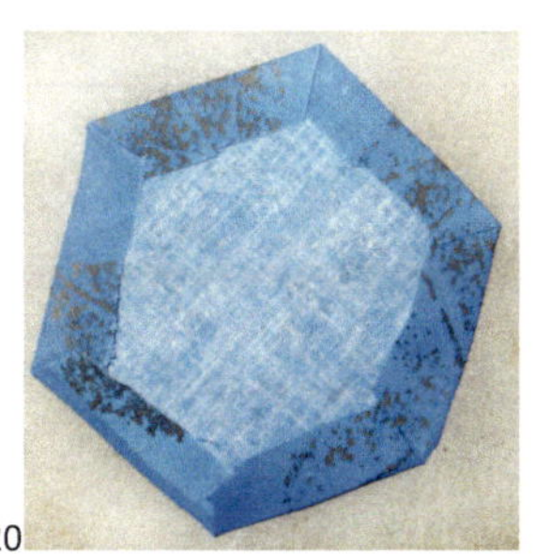
20

20. Gently remove the template from each lining piece. Press again if necessary.

21, 22. Place a lining side wrong sides together against the interfacing of a featured side. To sew:

21

22

– By Machine: Do a straight stitch 1/8 inch inside all the way around. This is illustrated on p.13.

– By Hand: Do this if there are beads. As you go, If the inner flaps on the squares' lining are long, tuck them in with your needle. A traditional whipstitch is the most visible; a ladder stitch, in photo 22 above, is the least obvious; a lacing stitch is in-between. All are explained on p. 10.

At the end, make a loop knot, then bury a knot as described in the middle of p. 9.

Join all the pieces

Machine stitchers: Use a wide zigzag to recreate the net on p. 30. Follow the procedure on p. 11 until the center is surrounded.

23. Hand stitchers: Surround the central piece to recreate the net on p. 30. Bring the center piece, and one of its surrounding pieces, together. Flip the second piece onto the first, featured sides together. You may want to use a clip to hold pieces in position.

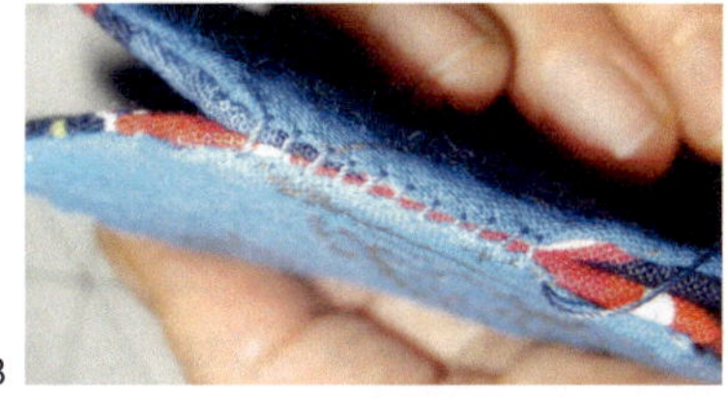
23

At the beginning of their mutual seam, bury a knot between the layers, and take a tiny stitch or two to secure it. Then use a traditional whipstitch or lacing stitch on p. 10 to join these layered pieces. Here I did a traditional whipstitch, but in this situation I also like the lacing stitch. In principle, I want to penetrate only the two featured sides that meet; but sometimes you can't avoid catching the linings. It's not a problem. But do avoid penetrating the interfacing, only because it's much harder to sew. (If you catch it by mistake, you don't have to unsew.)

24. At the first corner, do an extra tacking stitch. Bring the thread through the base, and flip the next piece in the formation on top of the central piece. Sew on.

continued

24

25. When all pieces are attached to the center, sew up the seams between the sides. You'll have to squish your dish in new and exciting ways. Don't worry – you won't hurt it!

26. Finish with a loop stitch and a knot, shown on p. 9.

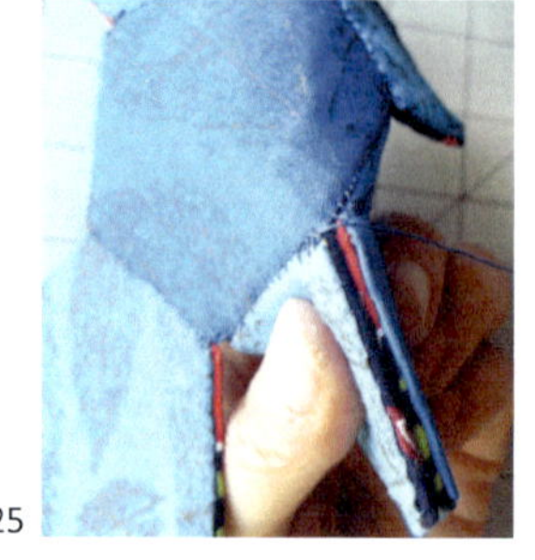

25

Geode Flap Finish

To make a flap that opens, choose one hexagon to serve as the lid, and stitch only one edge of it to the rest of the form.

Project 5 = Desktop Planetarium

This bowl was made from the same large net as the geode, and followed the same steps as on pp. 22-26. But instead of individually lining each piece, I did a duplicate whole lining, for a more polished exterior.
Here's how:

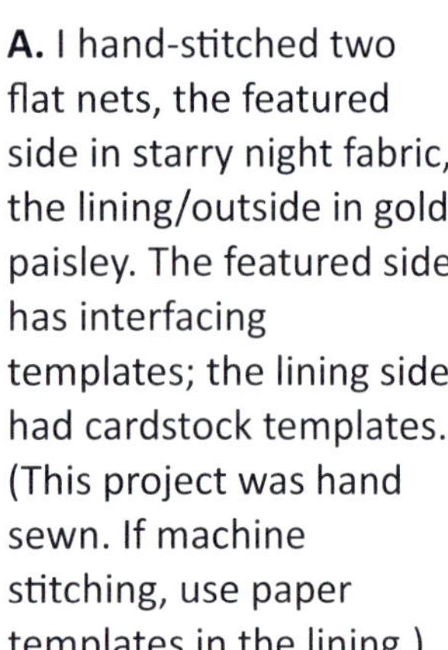

A. I hand-stitched two flat nets, the featured side in starry night fabric, the lining/outside in gold paisley. The featured side has interfacing templates; the lining side had cardstock templates. (This project was hand sewn. If machine stitching, use paper templates in the lining.)

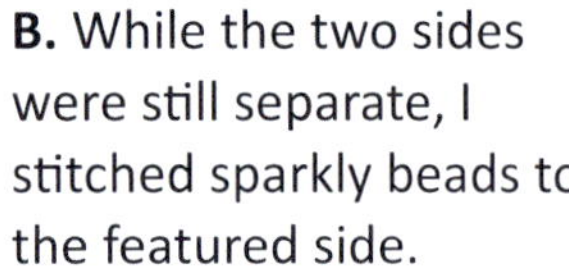

B. While the two sides were still separate, I stitched sparkly beads to the featured side.

C. I stitched the seams between pieces to pull each shape into the third dimension. Then I removed the cardstock templates from the lining.

D. I inserted the lining side into the featured side, wrong sides together, and stitched them together around the rim.

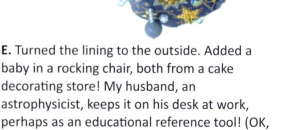

E. Turned the lining to the outside. Added a baby in a rocking chair, both from a cake decorating store! My husband, an astrophysicist, keeps it on his desk at work, perhaps as an educational reference tool! (OK, perhaps not so educational– it's comic relief!)

Project 6 = Beehive Hexagon Purse

While playing with my beaded geode, I discovered that if I flipped the beaded side out, and smushed the top edges together, pulling the flap forward, the result was an unusual purse!

So I made one on purpose!

The outer green print features bumblebees, script, and hexagons. There's a whole-project gold lining, and a flap with a closure. It uses 11 of the truncated octahedron's 14 pieces – 7 hexagons and 4 squares. When closed, like in the photo, it measures about 7.5" across x 4" high (not counting the handle). Its nets are on the right.

Materials

– Fabric There are two shapes in this polyhedron: squares and hexagons. So I chose two prints for the outside – a green one for hexagons, and gold one for squares. Two more gold prints were used for the lining.

– **Cardstock** If hand-sewing the lining; paper if machine-sewing it.

– Fusible interfacing For the exterior pieces, plus the inner flap

– Purse closure A two-part magnetic snap closure is ideal

– Purse ring. O ring, or bangle bracelet to serve as the handle

See also supplies on p. 3

You may want to make a paper model first, following this net, taping the shapes you print out from p. 30 (small) or pp.31-32 (large). Jot notes on the paper model to ensure directional fabrics are oriented correctly. "Down" in these diagrams means that edge faces the floor when carrying the purse.

1. Net for outer/ green side (good side of fabric)

2. Net for inner/lining/gold side (good side of fabric)

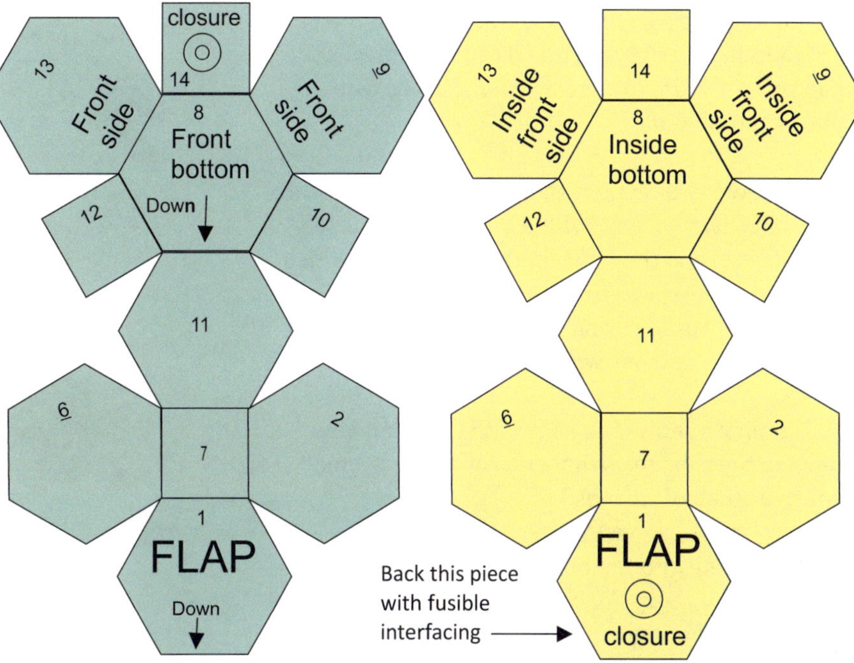

1,2. Print out one copy of the net on paper. Use one of each paper shape to cut 7 hexagons and 4 squares from fusible interfacing (see p. 5, method 2 for cutting interfacing). These will be the permanent templates for the outside.

Then cut one more hexagon from fusible interfacing. This eighth template will go behind the flap closure on the inner lining side. The rest of the lining pieces will have temporary templates.

3, 4. Construct the outer side. Use the fusible interfacing pieces to cut fabric 1/4" - 1/2" larger than each template all the way around.

At the ironing board, baste the fabric around the fusible interfacing. (See p. 8, method 3.)

Hand or machine stitch the pieces together to replicate the net above left. Photo 3 shows the outer side's front, and 4 shows its reverse side with all the pieces basted, and stitched into position. Machine stitching basics are on p. 11; hand stitching basics are on pp. 9-10.

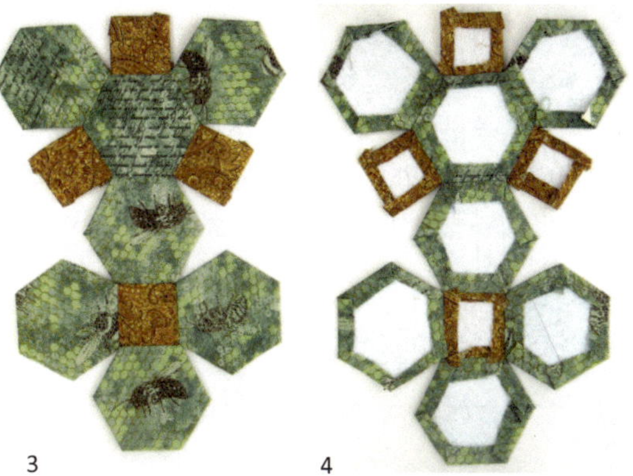

3 4

continued

Beehive Hexagon Purse, continued

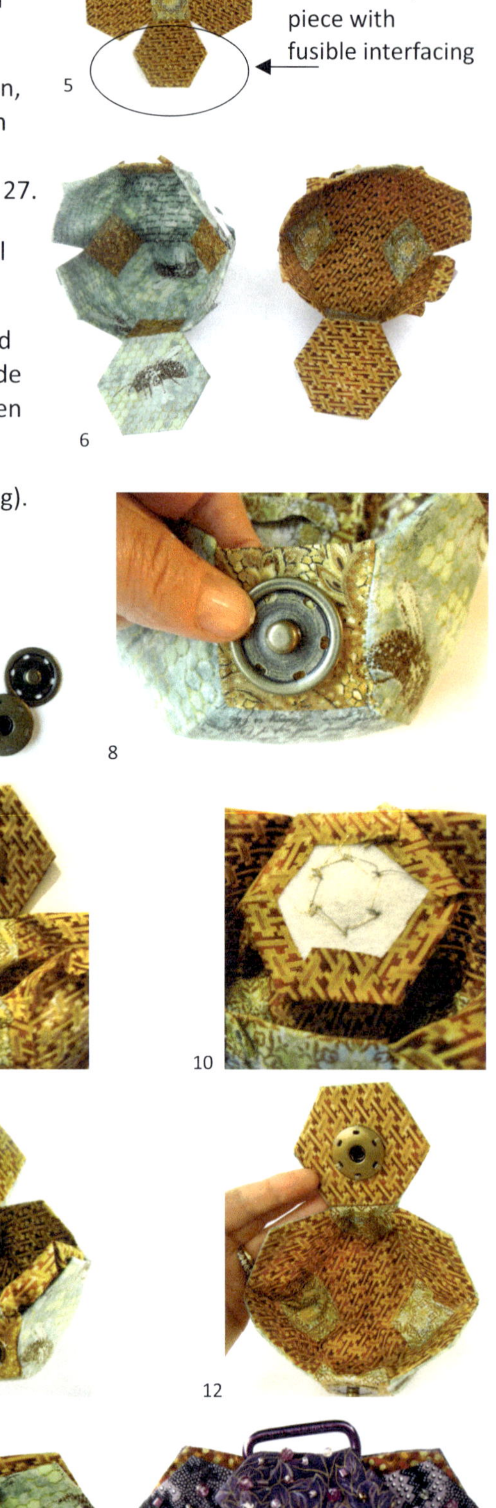

5. Construct the inside. Its templates will be temporary, except the flap, which should be backed with fusible interfacing.

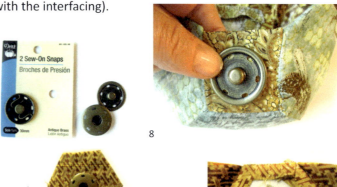

- If you'll join lining pieces mostly by machine, print out paper templates.
- If joining them by hand, print templates on cardstock. (Or, print on paper and then glue or trace to cardstock).

Use paper or cardstock templates (plus your one extra fusible interfacing hexagon, from step 2) of each shape, to cut out all the fabric pieces 1/4" - 1/2" bigger than the template all the way around. Baste each fabric piece around the templates. Stitch the pieces together (by hand or machine, pp. 9-11) to create the net on p. 27.

6. For both sides, once the net is complete, stitch the in-between seams that pull each half into the third dimension. Choose a hand stitch on p. 10.

Or, you can machine stitch – most of the way. I sewed both sides by machine, and got pretty far – in photo 6, you can see there was just one open seam on each side that I couldn't maneuver into the machine (the open seam on the left of the green side, and right on the gold side.) I sewed that last seam by hand on both units.

Remove all the templates from the inner side (except the flap with the interfacing).

7. Add a closure. I chose a 30mm brass snap from Dritz. It looks good, but now I have to smash the purse to shut it. In hindsight, I wish I'd chosen a magnetic snap purse closure instead – it shuts easily, with no smashing required.

8, 9. Follow the directions that come with the closure. It will have two halves. Put the outie on the purse's front square, and the innie on the inside flap. With a magnetic closure, you'll cut slits for the prongs. For this sew-in snap, I used strong grey beading thread, then covered those stitches with gold thread.

10. The photo shows the back of the top flap after stitching the closure. (With a magnetic clasp, you'll see prongs instead of stitches.)

11. Place lining into the outside, wrong sides together.

12. Stitch all the way around the rim and flap. A traditional whipstitch or ladder stitch works well (see p. 10.)

13, 14. This purse can be used as a clutch. Or add a handle. The one in the photo on top of p. 27 came from a thrift shop purse. On the beaded geode purse, I added a purple caribiner clip. You can even use a bangle bracelet!

Just slip the flap through the ring, and it's done!

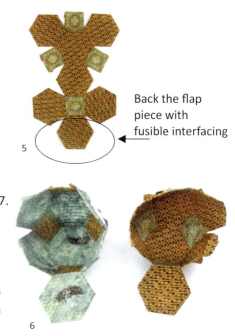

Project 7 = Play with Your Food or Cat Ball

Materials

- **Fabric** Small amounts. The ball pictured used two prints, one for the hexagons, another for the squares
- **Cardstock**
- **Stuffing**

See also supplies on p. 3

There's so much food fabric out there! I have fabric celebrating everything from asparagus to zucchini. One looks like matzoh, the cracker associated with the Jewish holiday of Passover.* Use food fabric that's meaningful to your giftee – it's such a fun holiday gift/ornament/toy!

There's even **more** cat and dog fabric out there. Andrea Shlasko used this pattern to make many creature-themed truncated octahedra, including the hilarious "Blah Blah Cats" ball on top of p. 22.

For the squares, I used a contrasting dark print. If you want to use more than two fabrics, you may want to map fabric placement on a paper model first (p. 4 explains why).

1. The large templates I used, on pp. 31-32, create a ball about 5.5" across; with small templates, p. 30, it will be closer to 4". Print the net onto cardstock if you're hand sewing; or paper if you'll machine sew. Cut the printed net apart. If you'll be centering printed motifs, see the fussy cutting directions on p. 6.

Place each template on the fabric, and cut all the way around, 1/4" - 1/2" bigger on all sides.

2. Baste each piece around the template, using the glue stick or hand-stitching methods on pp. 7-8.

3. Arrange the pieces like the net on p. 30. By hand, sew pieces right sides together with one of the stitches on p. 10. Machine sewing directions are on p. 11.

4, 5. Once net is completed, stitch remaining seams. By hand, work wrong side out. As the form curls, machine-stitchers will soon have to switch to hand-sewing from the wrong side. Hand and machine stitchers should work from closed toward open areas.

6. When only 2-4 unstitched edges are left, remove templates, and turn the form right side out.

7. Use a finger or chopstick to push the corner dimples outwards. Stuff well, and sew up the opening with tiny hand stitches. I suggest a ladder or lacing stitch (p. 10.) Play ball!

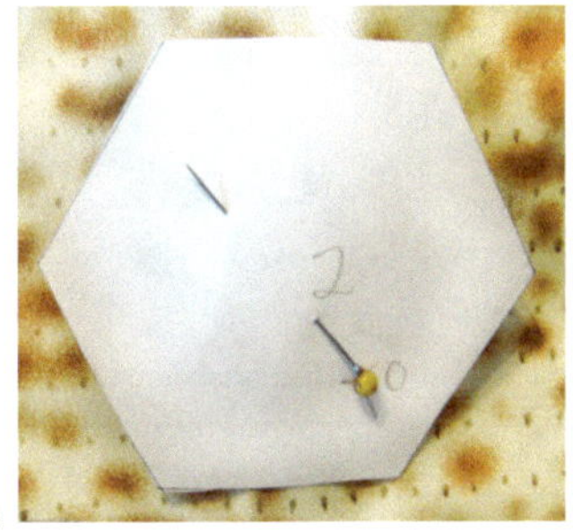

1

2

3

4

5

6

7

---

*I buy matzoh fabric from 1-800-dreidel.com, or www.faynicolljudaicadesigns.com.

Small Truncated Octahedron Net

The full polyhedron has a total of 14 sides; 8 are hexagons, and 6 are much smaller squares. With these small templates, the ball will measure about 4" at the widest.

Basic bowl: For a hexagon-centered bowl, use only Unit 1 (above the red line) or Unit 2 (below it). They're the same.

Square-centered bowl: Put a square in the middle, and sew a hexagon to each of the four sides. (For example, piece 7 surrounded by 1, 2, 11, and 6).

Geode, purse, other open shape: Make a paper model to decide how many pieces you want. My geode and purse left out pieces 3, 4 and 5.

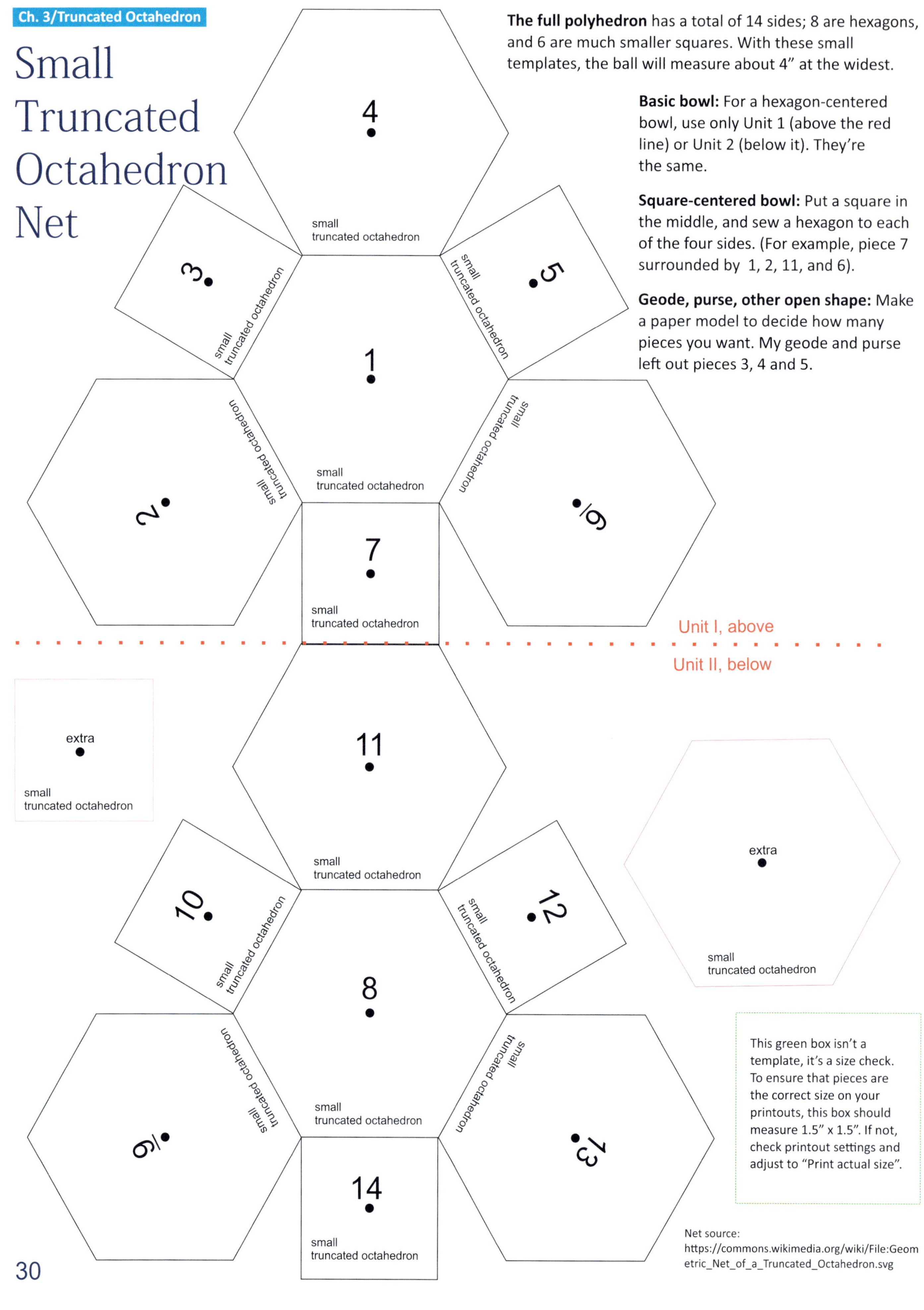

Net source: https://commons.wikimedia.org/wiki/File:Geometric_Net_of_a_Truncated_Octahedron.svg

Large Truncated Octahedron Net

The full polyhedron has a total of 14 sides; 8 are hexagons and 6 are much smaller squares. Combine **Unit 1** on this page with **Unit II** on the next to make it. You'll join piece 7 on this page to piece 11 on the next. The complete polyhedron will measure about 5.5" at its widest.

Bowls Possibilities are explained on top of p. 30.

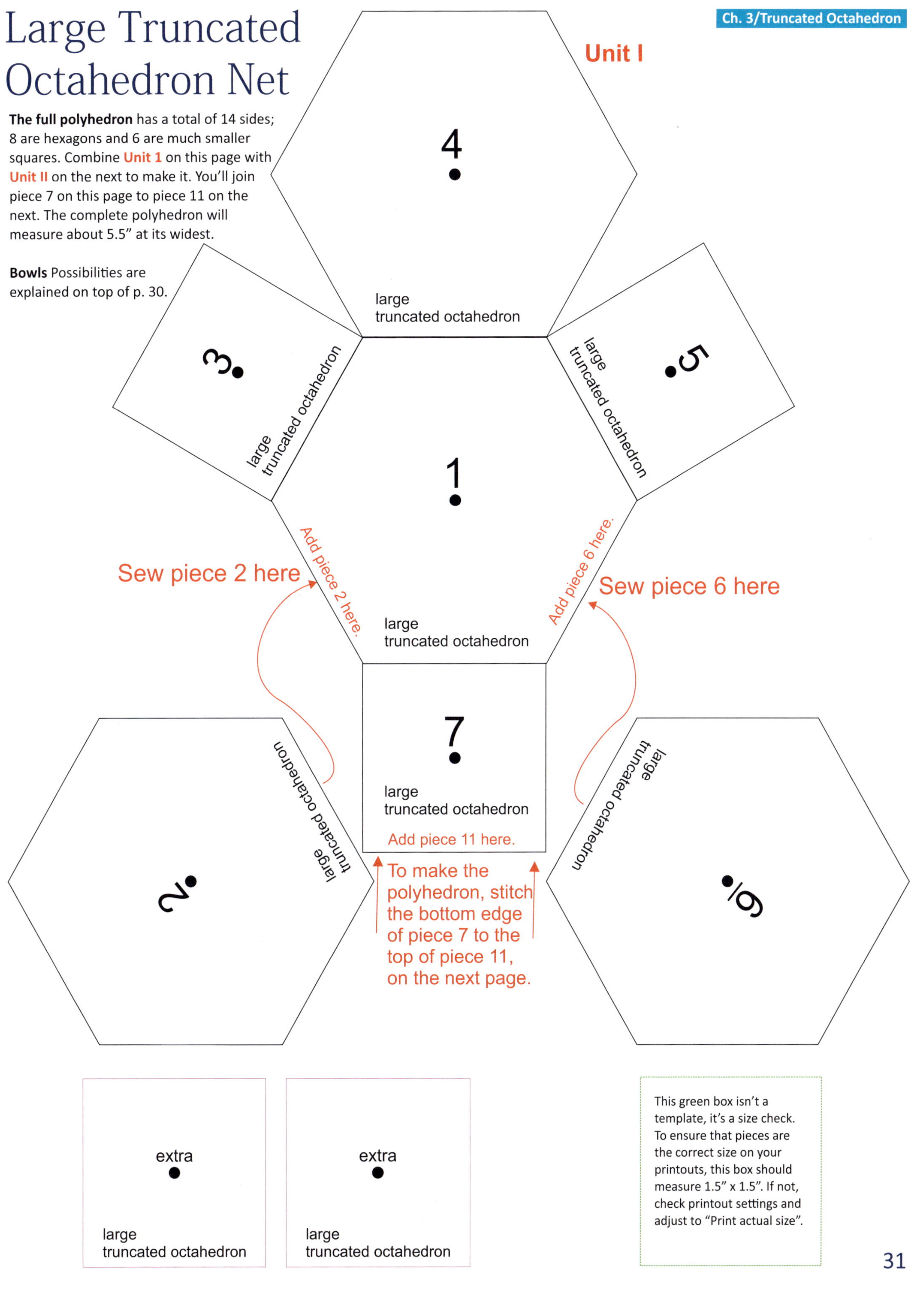

This green box isn't a template, it's a size check. To ensure that pieces are the correct size on your printouts, this box should measure 1.5" x 1.5". If not, check printout settings and adjust to "Print actual size".

Large Truncated Octahedron Net

Unit II

Joining Unit I to Unit II is explained on top of the previous page.

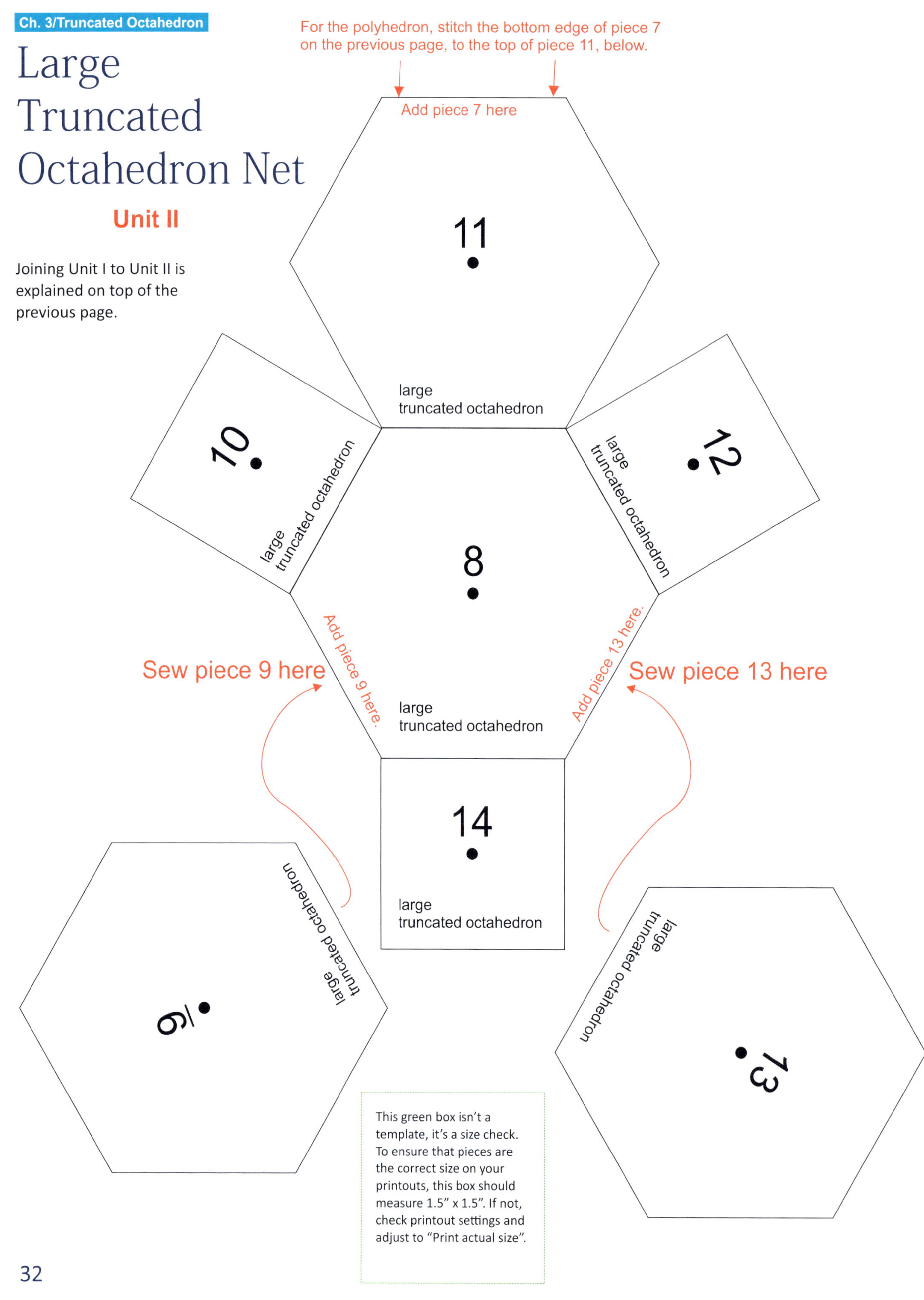

This green box isn't a template, it's a size check. To ensure that pieces are the correct size on your printouts, this box should measure 1.5" x 1.5". If not, check printout settings and adjust to "Print actual size".

Ch. 4/Truncated Cuboctahedron

This is an easy one, too. The polyhedron has three shapes: 12 squares, 8 hexagons, and 6 octagons. The big flat octagons make it unlikely to roll – so it's a good pincushion! For fun, I embroidered midlines through the largest faces. Made with small templates, it's about 3.5" high, not counting pins!

Just 9 pieces creates a shallow bowl that's easy to machine sew. For something asymmetrical, build up one or two sides. The purple form on the far right is a 13-piece "geode". I cut an oval in one piece to serve as a handle. Explore ideas with a paper model first. Templates are on pp. 37-39.

Polka dot ball by Glenise Gallagher

Project 8 = Laced Candy Dish

Materials

– Featured side Big bag of truffles (or any interesting wrappers).

– Cardstock for templates; or for much stronger templates use cardboard or Kraft-Tex™ (see p. 5).

– Strong thread Upholstery thread or beading silamide are good choices.

– Glue stick

See also supplies on p. 3

An outer candy bag, plus 4 individual wrappers from the chocolates inside, were used to make this bowl. The top view is on the left, the bowl's bottom on the right. I punched holes with an unthreaded needle in my machine, and hand-laced through them. The inner templates remain in place permanently.

1. Purchase the largest possible bag of chocolates. Yes, this project is tough. Save individual wrappers and the bag they came in. I shared the chocolates at a party and followed guests around to collect their wrappers. It's a great way to meet people and convince them you're crazy.

2. Print the large net, unit 1 from p. 38, onto cardstock. Finished large bowl will measure about 5.5" x 2". Cut out pieces 1-9.

With cardboard or **Kraft-Tex™ only**: Print the net on paper; cut out one of each shape; and use those to cut the 9 shapes from the cardboard or Kraft-Tex™. See p. 5, method 3 .You may not need to make lining pieces – cardboard or **Kraft-Tex™** can double as inside and back side.

3. Use the octagonal template to cut out the two sides of the base piece from the candy bag. The featured side, photo 2, will face up in the bowl. Cut so it extends 1/2" beyond the template on all sides (photo 1). The lining side, photo 3, should be cut the same size as the template. It will wind up facing down to the table. (Or, with Kraft-Tex™ or cardboard, you may not want this third base piece.)

1

2

3

continued

Laced dish, continued

4. Place the template, then the octagonal lining, inside the back of the featured side, and fold the sides over it. Glue isn't necessary – edges will soon be held by stitching.

5. Use square templates to cut four featured sides – each about 1/2" bigger, all the way around. Then cut four lining pieces that are the same size as the templates (unless you only want two layers).

4

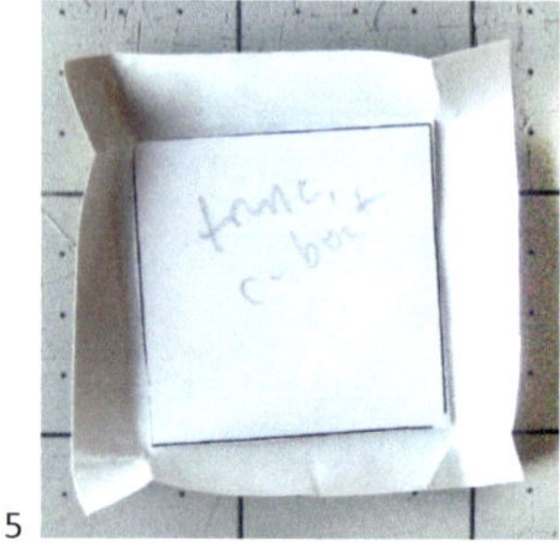
5

It's vital to include nutrition information to counteract the chocolate cravings this bowl will inspire!

6. Place the template, then the lining sides inside the featured side, with the good side of the lining facing up. (Or skip the back piece if you're okay with the template showing.) Fold the edges in. Again, glue isn't necessary – soon we'll stitch.

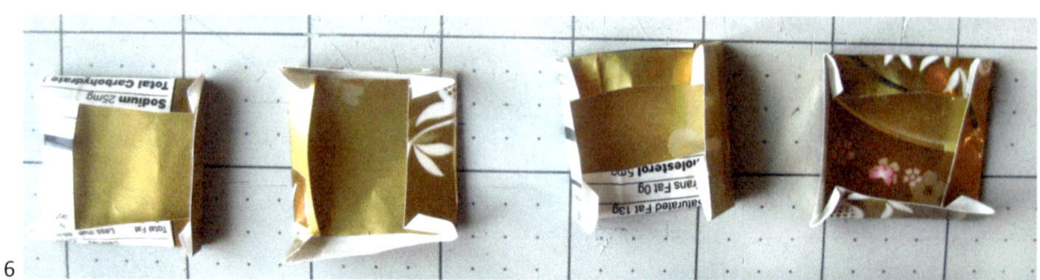
6

7, 8, 9. Wrap candy wrappers around the hexagonal templates. These templates will also stay in place permanently. Photos 7-9 show the wrap that worked for me with this particular candy.

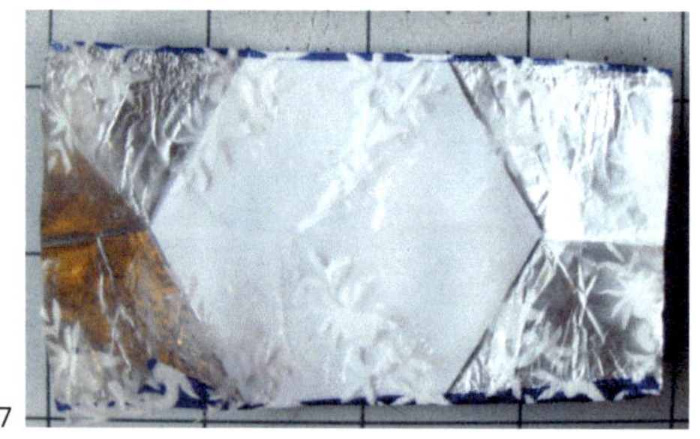
7

8

10, 11. From the back, stitch an X across each hexagon to hold the folds in place. I used gold metallic thread. Photo 10 shows where I stitched. Photo 11 shows the front.

9

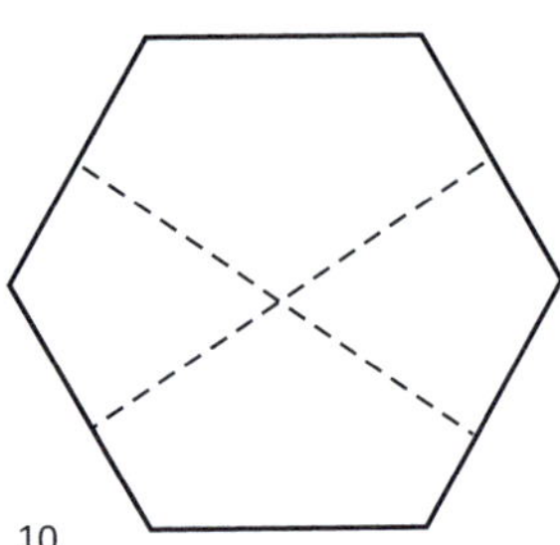
10

11

12. Lay the pieces out good side up, next to the sewing machine, following the net.

13. I was concerned that the paper and foil would cut my sewing machine thread. So I just used the machine to poke holes, instead.

Set machine for a long stitch. Unthread the top and bobbin. "Sew" a straight stitch all the way around each piece, 1/4" in from the edge. If you're not sure whether you want rim stitching, punch holes only around 3 of the 4 square sides, and only 5 of the 6 hexagon sides. You can add rim holes later if you like. Punch holes around all 8 octagon sides.

12

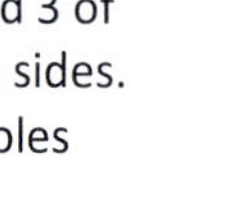

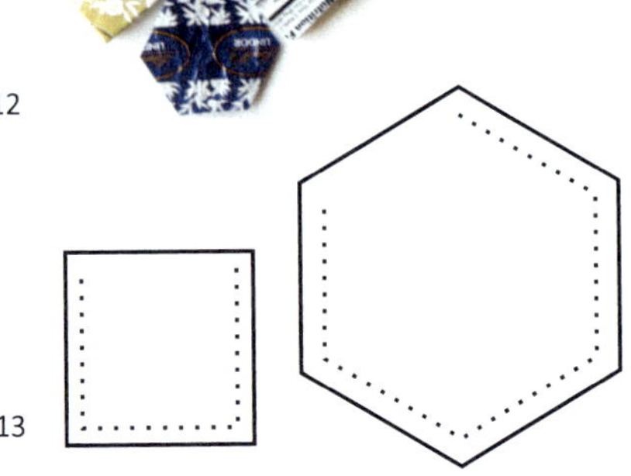

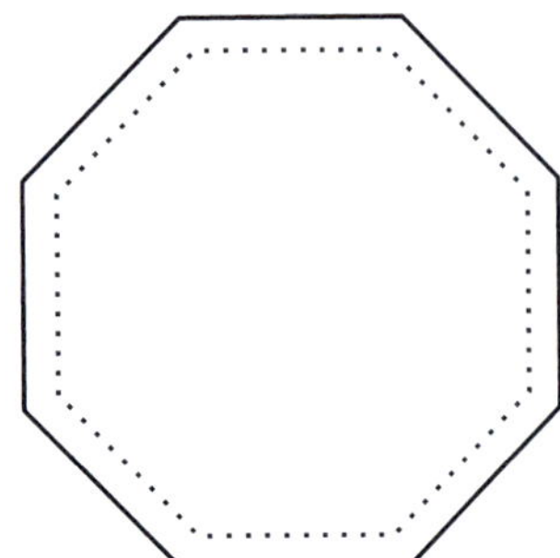
13

continued

14. Tie a knot in strong thread. Send the needle into a seam allowance on back, and poke it straight into the fold, creating a new, small hole to catch the knot.

I used a lacing stitch. Working from the top, bring the needle up through the gap between pieces, then send it down into the first hole in the right (blue) side, at 1. Bring it up through the gap again, and bring it down into the hole 2 on the pink side. Up through the middle again, and go into hole 3 on the blue side. Up through the gap, and down into 4. Keep going. I wasn't shy about skipping a hole, or even poking a new one if necessary.

15. I took two stitches at the end of every piece, before moving onto the next one.

16. Join all 9 pieces as shown.

17. Stitch up the sides. Start with a knot hidden inside a seam allowance. At the end of each side. do a loop knot or two (p. 9) and clip inside the seam allowance.

18. If you want decorative stitching around the rim, punch holes with your sewing machine (if you didn't do it earlier). Here I did a hand whipstitch through the holes, with gold metallic thread.

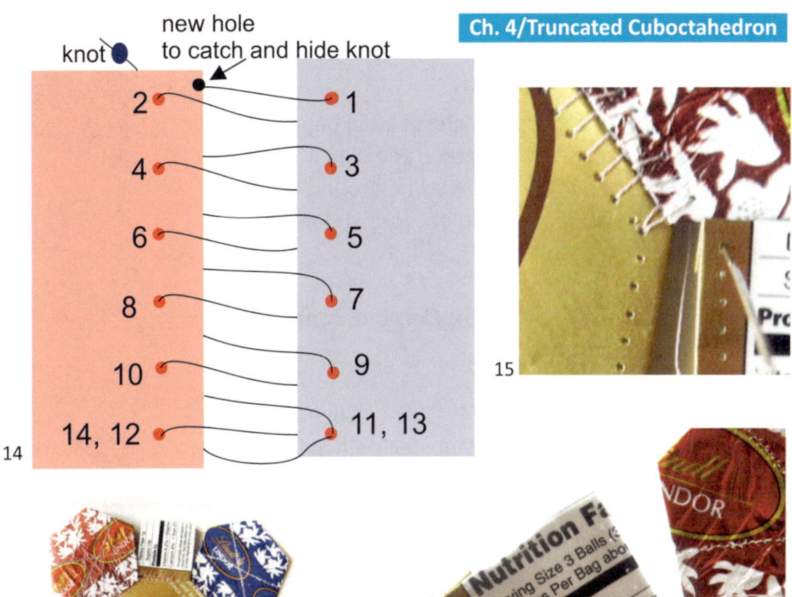

14

15

16

17

18

Project 9 = Laurel's Quick Dish

Materials

- **Fabric** Small amounts
- **Stiff fusible interfacing**
- **Thread:** Decorative or invisible sewing machine thread
- **Glue stick**

See also supplies on p. 3

This dish has the same configuration as the candy wrapper dish, but goes much faster, since it's entirely stitched by machine. I suggest you use the large net (p. 38) for easiest construction and a bowl that measures about 5.5" wide and 2" high.

1, 2. Choose featured side fabrics. I used two colorful Laurel Burch prints: One with birds, for the hexagons, and one with flowers and cats for the squares and the central octagon.

For the lining side (the bottom, which faces down to the table), we're going to do a raw-edge finish. But if you prefer a turned edge lining or whole-piece lining, see p. 12-13.

1

2

continued

Laurel's dish, continued

3. Print the net on paper. Take one of each paper shape – a square, hexagon, and octagon – and clip it to stiff fusible interfacing. Option: Draw a line around it if that will help you cut accurately. Cut out four squares, four hexagons, and one octagon.

4. If you want to fussy-cut pieces like I did, centering flowers, see options on p. 6.

5. Cut out the fabric pieces, 1/4" - 1/2" from each template, all the way around. (You decide what size seam allowance you like best.)

6. Center interfacing shapes on the back of fabric pieces. With 1-sided fusible interfacing: The fusible side should face up from the back.

Turn all featured fabric edges to the back side, and fuse or glue in place. (See pp. 7-8.)

7, 8. Photo 7 shows the backs, and 8 shows the fronts.

9. Choose a lining method from those on p.12-13. For this casual bowl, I chose the raw edge lining (p. 12, method 2).

Using the front pieces as templates, cut shapes out of backing fabric(s). I picked yellow for squares, green for hexagons, and red for the octagon. Fuse and/or glue stick them to the backs of all the featured side pieces. Even if the interfacing has fusible on that side, you'll need to glue around the edges, so the lining clings to the featured fabric flaps turned from the front.

10. Arrange the pieces as you want them in your bowl.

11. For machine stitching: Load machine with decorative thread. I used a gold metallic on top and in the bobbin.

Place the central piece and one of its surrounding pieces under the foot.

Follow the directions on p. 11 to surround the central piece with the side squares and hexagons. Next, stitch up the side seams, to pull the bowl into the third dimension. Photo 12 shows the finished back.

Finish with a zigzag or decorative stitch around the rim.

If you prefer to hand-stitch, choose from the stitches on p. 10.

3 4 5 6 7 8 9 10 11 12

Small Truncated Cuboctahedron Net

This size is small, to fit on one page, but it's doable in fabric. Unless you're new to EPP – in that case, use the large size for your first stitched project

Full polyhedron: 26 pieces: 12 squares, 8 hexagons, 6 octagons. Finished size is about 3.5" at its widest. This is the size used for the pincushion pictured on top of p. 33

Simple bowl: Inside the red dotted lines, pieces 1-9 or pieces 13-21 (they're the same).

Alternative bowl: Start with piece 10 in the middle. Surround it with a pair of hexagons (9 and 17) on opposite sides, and a pair of octagons (11 and 12) on the remaining sides. This layout is inside the blue dotted lines.

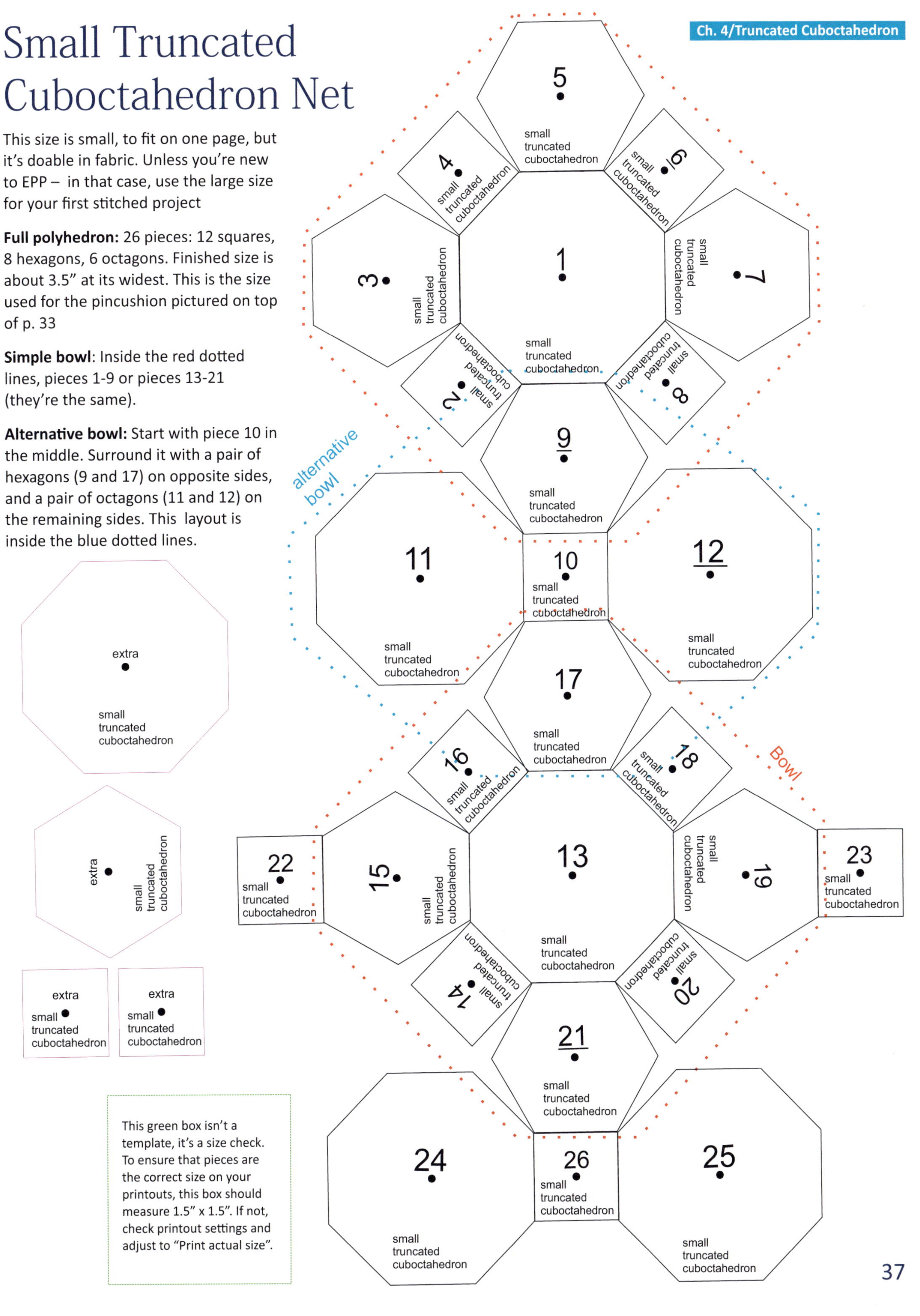

This green box isn't a template, it's a size check. To ensure that pieces are the correct size on your printouts, this box should measure 1.5" x 1.5". If not, check printout settings and adjust to "Print actual size".

Large Truncated Cuboctahedron Net

Full polyhedron: 26 pieces; 12 squares, 8 hexagons, and 6 octagons. Connect this page's Unit 1 of the net to Unit II on the next page. The polyhedron will measure about 5.5" at the widest.

Bowls: Possibilities are explained on the previous page. This large size is easier to construct than the small one.

This green box isn't a template, it's a size check. To ensure that pieces are the correct size on your printouts, this box should measure 1.5" x 1.5". If not, check printout settings and adjust to "Print actual size".

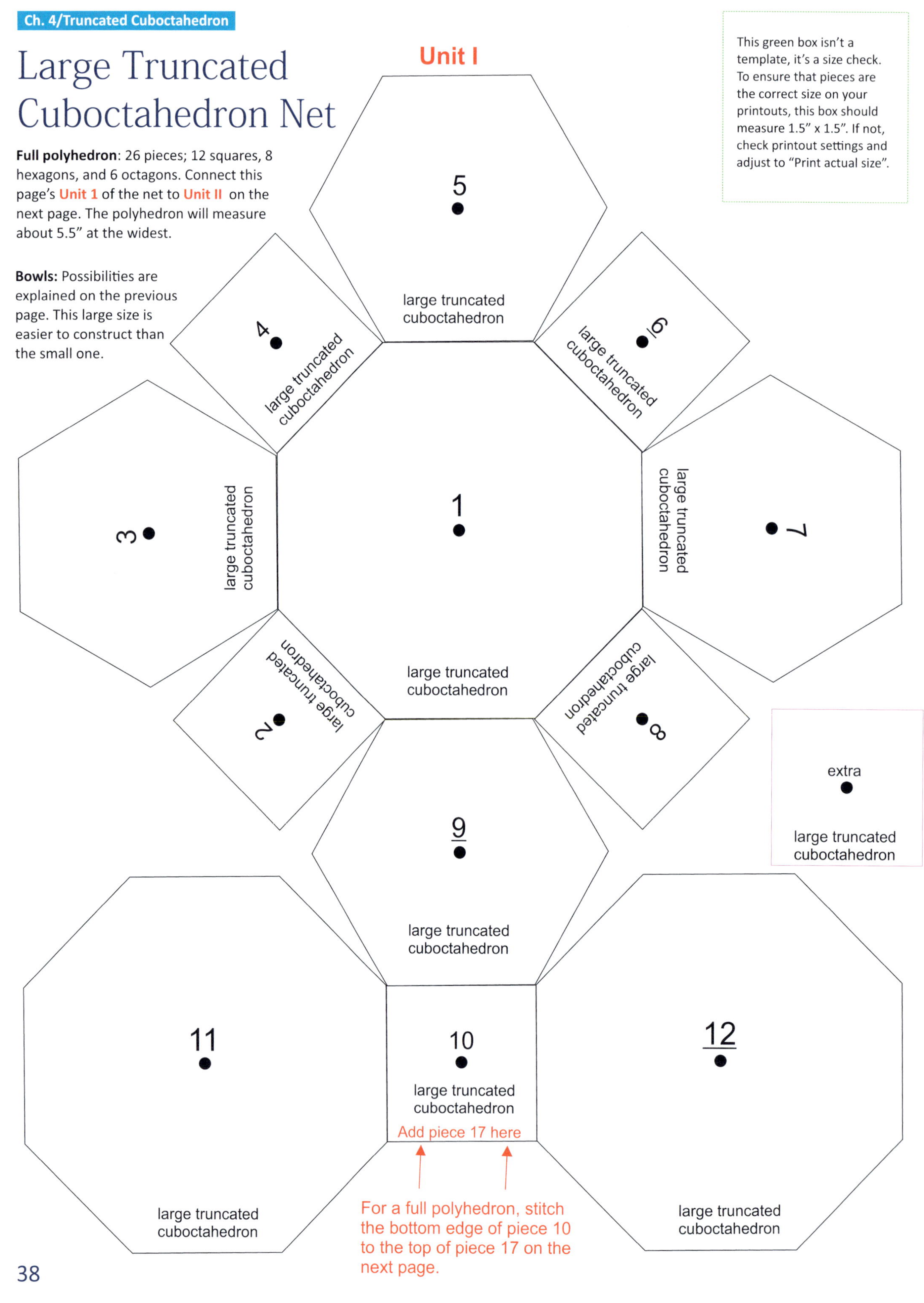

Large Truncated Cuboctahedron Net

See assembly information on previous page.

Unit II

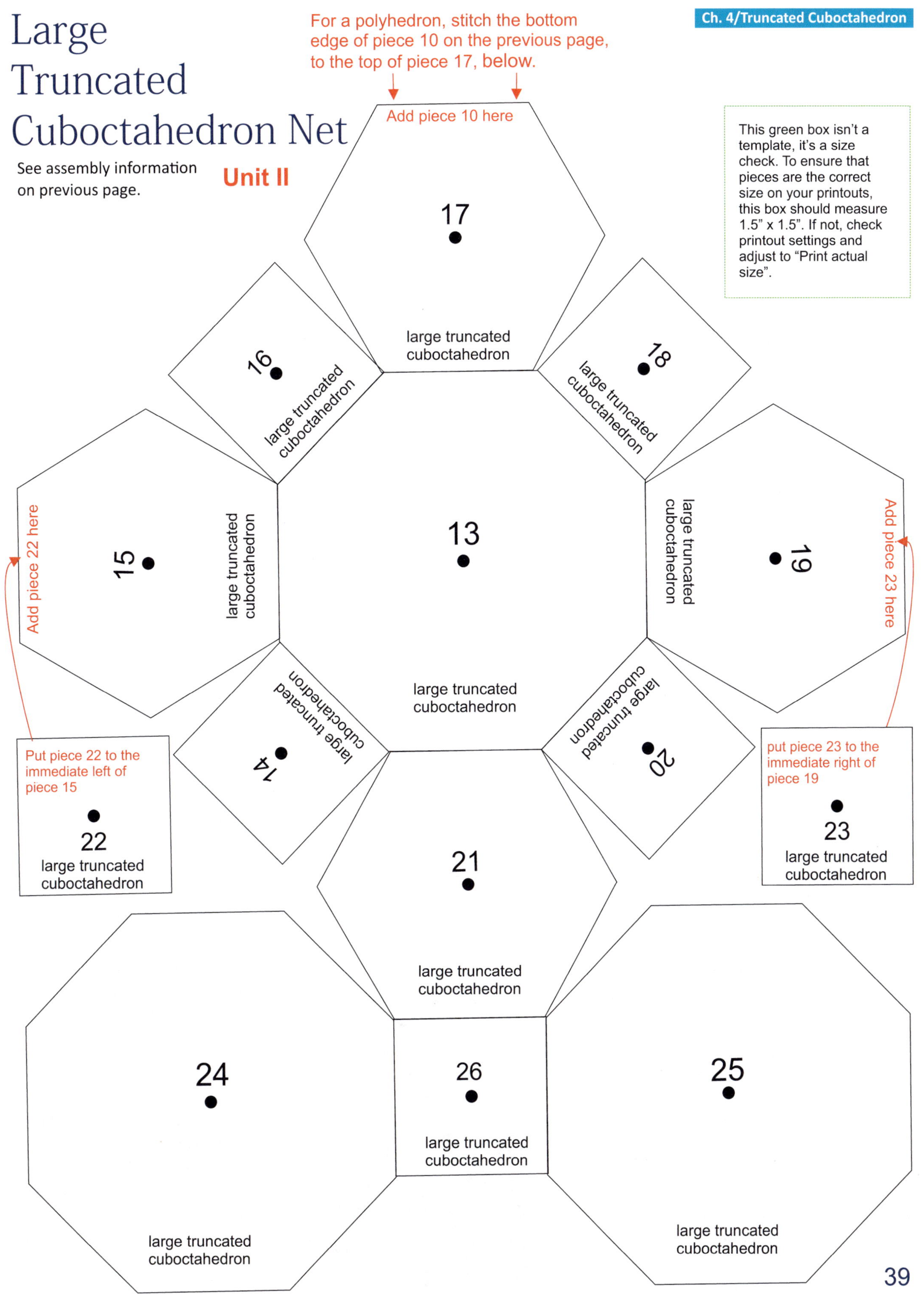

Ch. 5/Icosahedron

All 20 pieces in this polyhedron are triangles, but this isn't a beginners' project. Basting triangles is trickier than other shapes.

On the upside, the net is easy to understand, if you think of it as containing the three subunits marked on the right: a lid, a side strip, and a base. The lid and base are pieced identically. This idea makes it easy to brainstorm variations.

With no lid, it's a convertible basket – it can sit at an angle with its base popped down, or straight up like any other basket with the base popped up. Sew the "lid" on permanently and stuff it, for an unusual pillow. In the project below, we install a zipper between the lid and base, so it became a wristlet/purse.

The full, closed icosahedron can be sewn entirely by hand, or about two-thirds of the way by machine. For the purse, you can join all the side pieces by machine; but sewing that strip to the base will require determined hand sewing!

Project 10 = Zippered Icosa-Case

Use the large templates on p. 48. This purse will wind up about 9" from point to opposite point. We will line each piece individually.

1. Plan fabrics for the top, bottom and sides, outside and in. A paper model is very helpful (p. 4). To show off the triangular faces, consider alternating contrasting fabrics in the side strip. Or maybe use one fabric on the lid, and the other on the base, to distinguish them, as in diagram 1.

2. Print the large templates onto cardstock. Cut out one triangle, and use it to trace and cut out 20 same-size triangles from stiff fusible interfacing (p. 5, method 2.)

1

Lay each interfacing triangle on the outer fabric(s) and cut out the fabric, 1/4" - 1/2" bigger than the interfacing all the way around. If you don't need to fussy-cut, you can cut a bunch at once with a rotary cutter and ruler. (If you do want to fussy-cut printed motifs, see p. 6).

Baste the fabric triangles to the interfacing, using the procedure in the box on the next page.

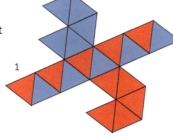

2

Materials

– **Outer fabric** Fat-quarter or quarter - yard of one; or less of each if you use two contrasting fabrics.

– **Inside fabric** Fat-quarter or quarter yard. To disguise seams, choose fabric with a similar color and value as the outside.

– **Stiff fusible interfacing**

– **Cardstock** For temporary templates behind the inner side.

– **Purse hardware** 1 lightweight swivel hook; one decorative ring for the lid tip.

– **Strong hand-sewing thread** Upholstery, quilting, or other strong thread to join pieces. Thick craft or embroidery thread to attach ring.

– **Zipper** With large-size templates, buy a 20" zipper.

See also supplies on p. 3

continued

How to baste triangles

This applies to any triangle in this book. At the ironing board, use parchment paper or an appliqué press sheet to keep fusible from smearing the board and/or iron. If the interfacing has fusible on one side only, place that side facing up at you from the back. If there's fusible on both sides, place the slightly smoother side facing down against the back of the featured fabric. **This same folding procedure can also be used with cardstock templates**. Just apply glue as needed.

A. Place template on fabric, and cut out fabric 1/4" - 1/2" larger, all the way around. Trim to a scant 1/4" around the points, and cut each fabric tip flat across.(If both interfacing sides have fusible, press the front side first, with a press sheet underneath to protect the ironing board from the glue on back.)

B. On back, fold the fabric tip down and press/fuse in position. (With cardstock: Glue lightly).

C. Fold right or left flap in first and press. From now on, stick with that side first for all corners and all pieces in the same project, including lining pieces. Above, the left flap is folded in first (after the center flap). Press with iron's tip or edge, and use a glue stick between fabric layers if needed.

D. Fold the opposite flap in and fuse and/or glue. Don't press all the way down the fold, just within an inch or so of the top.

E. If either flap protrudes beyond the edges, snip off excess.

F. Rotate triangle and repeat: Turn down tip, turn in one side flap first (the same side you turned first in step C). Fold in opposite flap.With 3 corners finished, it looks like this. The points don't have to be perfectly pointy.

G. If there are still protrusions after trimming, you can tuck-and-hide them later, when you join the piece to its lining.

Zippered Case, continued

3. Use a cardstock template to cut out lining fabric. Cut 1/4" - 1/2" larger than the template all the way around, and trim points flat across, a scant 1/4" above the template's tips.

4. Print out enough cardstock templates to make 20 individual turned-under linings. (Use paper if you'll be machine stitching the lining). The spray starch method is a good choice (p. 7, method 2). Use just a little glue in corners. Follow the same edge-turning procedure as in the box above. Once each piece's edges are turned, glued, and pressed, gently remove templates, readjust corners that need it; and hit it with the iron again it to flatten everything.

(If you're on the road, you can use the method on bottom of p. 13 to fit each lining to a featured side and hand-stitch it in position.)

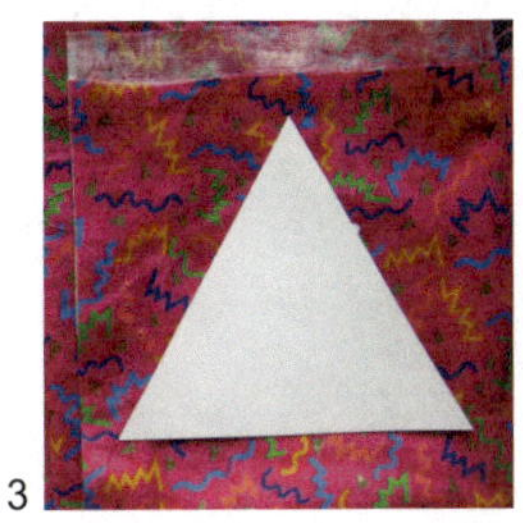

3

4

continued

Zippered Case, continued

5. Align each lining piece on the back of each featured side, and stitch together, using a stitch on p. 10 or p. 13. My favorite is a hand ladder stitch, p. 10.

6. Arrange the three subunits next to the sewing machine, following the net. The photo shows the lid, base, and side strip pieces just before they're put together.

Sew the subunits

7. Sew together the line of 10 triangles that make up the case's sides. I used a machine, but you can do this by hand if you prefer.

By machine: Test machine tension with samples of the same fabric covering interfacing scrap pieces. Use a wide zigzag. Keep length short, close to a satin stitch. Sew from the right side. Journey down the seams following the alphabet path. At each end, plant the needle in the last piece, lift presser foot and swivel the strip, so you're aiming down the next seam. Bring the next piece up against the previous one and stitch on. More machine sewing information is on p. 11.

By hand: Do one of the stitches on p. 10 – traditional whipstitch, Andrea's variation, a ladder stitch, or a lacing stitch – also following the back-and-forth alphabet path in diagram 7.

8. The photo shows a closeup of my machine zigzag.

9, 10. Join strip ends. By hand, you can sew with right sides together. By machine, work with right sides up. Photos 9 and 10 show how to butt the ends together, slide them into the machine, if you have a freearm, and stitch the join with a zigzag, starting and ending with a few tiny back-and-forth straight stitches. If you don't have a freearm, you may have to do this stitching inside the bottom of the ring (with good side facing into the circle). If that's too awkward, do it by hand!

11. Voila, the sides form a loop! (Lampshade?) Turn the ring good side out again, if it isn't already.

12. Assemble the base, and the lid. The obvious stitching order within each is to sew inward and then outward twice, as in the diagram, making two "V"s. By hand, sew right sides together. By machine, use a zigzag on top. Do some back- and-forth-tiny straight stitches at the beginning and end of each "V".

continued

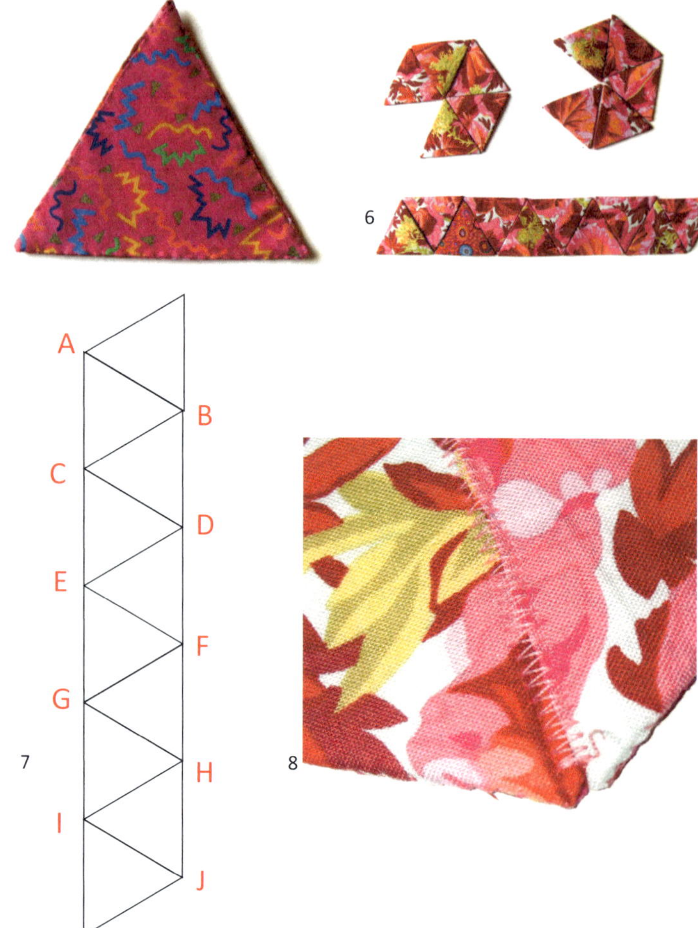

5
6
7
8

9

10

11

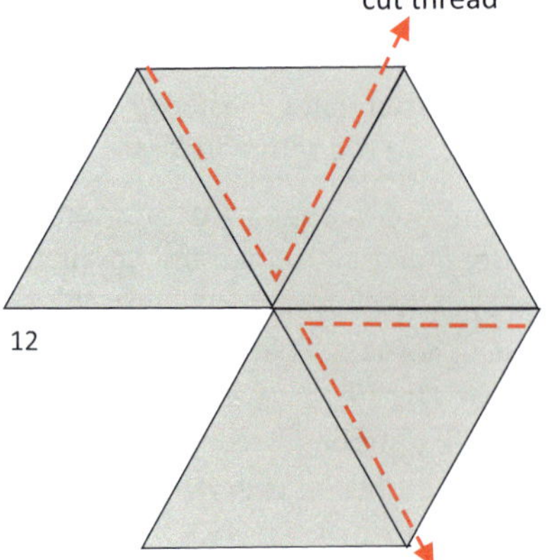

12

13, 14, 15, 16. Sew the last seam on the lid and base, to bring each into the third dimension.

To do this at the machine, I cup the unit upwards, so its central tip is the lowest point, and the outer edges rise up. Start with a few back-and-forth straight stitches on one side. Then center the pieces under the presser foot. Take 1-2 zigzags in place (photo 13). Move one stitch forward, and start bringing edges together (14). Do one more zigzag. By the second or third zigzag, the edges will want to snap together, so go with that (15). Sew carefully to the end, and do a few more straight stitches back and forth at the end.

Photo 16 shows the finished lid. Repeat to make the base.

17. Now you have a lid, base, and sides. If you like, you can change your mind and declare that the base is the lid and vice versa!

Join the three units

I have to do this by hand!

18, 19. Insert the base into the side ring, with good sides together. Photo 18 is a closeup of two edges lined up, ready to be sewn. Use a stitch on p. 10 to join them, all the way around. Photo 19 shows the base whipstitched in position, from the inside.

Intermission

20, 21 If you stop now, you have an interesting open basket /bowl/hat. It can sit straight up on a surface if you punch the base unit up and then slightly push its center a little down, as in the photos.

22, 23. Or, with the base fully extended downward, the basket tilts jauntily to one side.

Try resting the lid on top, photo 23. Unfortunately, it may be slightly smaller than the side unit, and tend to fall in. This project's solution: An easy zipper. It will hold the lid up on top of the basket, even when the zipper is open.

continued

13 14 15 16 17 18 19 20 21 22 23

Zippered case, continued

Install the Zipper

Zipper length should be 20” if you used large size templates. Work with the lining side out for the next several steps.

24. Make a tab to cover zipper ends. Cut a fabric rectangle 2.5” high x 3” wide.

25. Fold sides to the center and press.

26. Fold top edge down a quarter-inch (glue stick helps) and press.

27, 28. Decide which basket wall triangle will be the back. Pin the tab to the back panel, as shown. Unzip the zipper most of the way. Pin the base of the zipper onto the tab as shown, so the bottom row of teeth are just above the basket’s rim. (I’ve outlined the zipper end in black in photo 28.)

29, 30. Wrap the zipper around the top edge of the base, with teeth just slightly above the edge. Clip or pin in place as you go. When you reach the beginning, pin and trim off any part of the zipper end that overlaps the zipper beginning. (In photo 30 I have again outlined in black the bottom edge of the zipper tape.)

31, 32. Use strong thread to hand stitch the lower zipper tape in position. First do a line of running or back stitches *just* under the zipper teeth.

32, 33. At the end, go down a bit and sew around again, this time running your stitches just above the bottom edge of the zipper tape. Now you have a double row of stitching along the bottom zipper tape.

Add the Lid

34. Decide which lid triangle you want in back. Pin that rear panel directly above the rear panel of the basket wall, centered behind the tab. Again in this photo and the next one, I’ve outlined the base of the zipper.

35, 36. Pin the top zipper tape along the entire bottom edge of the lid, with its teeth extending just below the lid’s edge. At each corner there will be little gaps created by the zipper tape’s top edge. One is circled in photo 36.

24 25 26 27 28 29 30 31 32 33 34 35 36

continued

37. Snip off any part of the top zipper end that overlaps the top zipper tape beginning.

38. Sew the top zipper tape to the lid, just as you did before, with a running or backstitch. Do the first line of stitching just above the zipper teeth.

39, 40. Then stitch around again, just below the top edge of the tape. Take an extra stitch at corners (39), to bring in gaps.

Now there's four rounds of hand stitching on the zipper: two rows along the bottom tape, two along the top.

41. Fold up the bottom of the tab, and then fold the top down over it. Pin, then hand stitch in position.

42. You have a very nice zippered case! Doesn't it need something on top? Like a precious jewel, a pom pom, or a statement button?

43. Or how about a top ring and handle to make it a wristlet/purse? The hardware and software in the photo includes:

- A lightweight decorative purse ring stitched on top of the lid (for this photo, I temporarily used a black ring; I later changed to the retro clear lucite ring shown below).
- A swivel hook that clips to the ring
- A fabric leash handle to attach to one end of the swivel hook.

44. Here's the clear ring I preferred to the black one.

45. Load a needle with multi-strand embroidery thread, or thick craft thread, or anything sturdy. Knot the end.

46, 47. Starting inside the lid, in the center of one panel's tip, push the needle all the way through. Pull to the knot. Place the ring in position, then stitch downward into the middle of an opposite panel. Try not to stitch into the spaces between panels! Go around 3-4 times.

Inside, take a couple of small stitches. Then knot the thread a half inch from where it emerges - send the needle back in, travel it an inch away just under the top layer, pull it up and tug until the knot is buried. Cut thread close to wherever it emerges.

continued

Zippered case, continued

Make a Handle

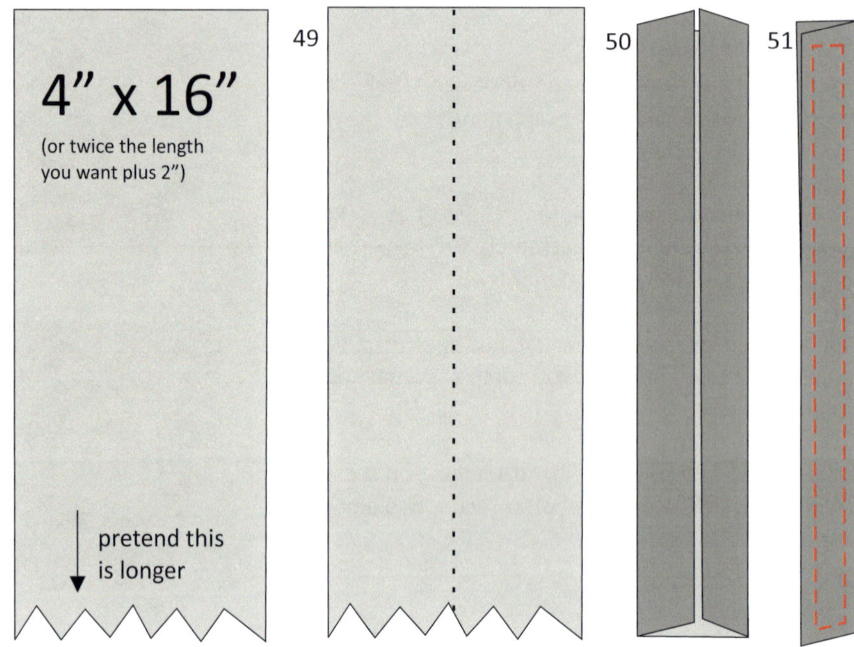

48. Start with a length of fabric that's 4" wide by 16" high. (Or twice the length you want, plus 2")

49. Fold in half the long way to crease the center.

50. Open, then fold the sides inward to touch the center fold, and press.

51. Fold in half the long way, and press again. Topstitch a rectangle as shown by the red dotted line.

52. Fold the top edge down 1/4".

53, 54. Fold it down again, this time 1" Slide a swivel hook's end ring onto the strap. Bring the bottom end up and slide it under the flap.

55. Stitch an x in a box as shown, to secure everything. Clip the swivel hook to the top ring! You're done!

Here the purse is seated straight up, with the base pushed upwards and inside. With the base pushed down, it will tilt.

Small Icosahedron Net

Full polyhedron: Twenty triangles. Finished polyhedron will measure about 4" from point to opposite point.

Bowl: Inside the red dotted line. 15 triangles make an interesting basket that tilts or stands up straight. See step 20 on p. 23.

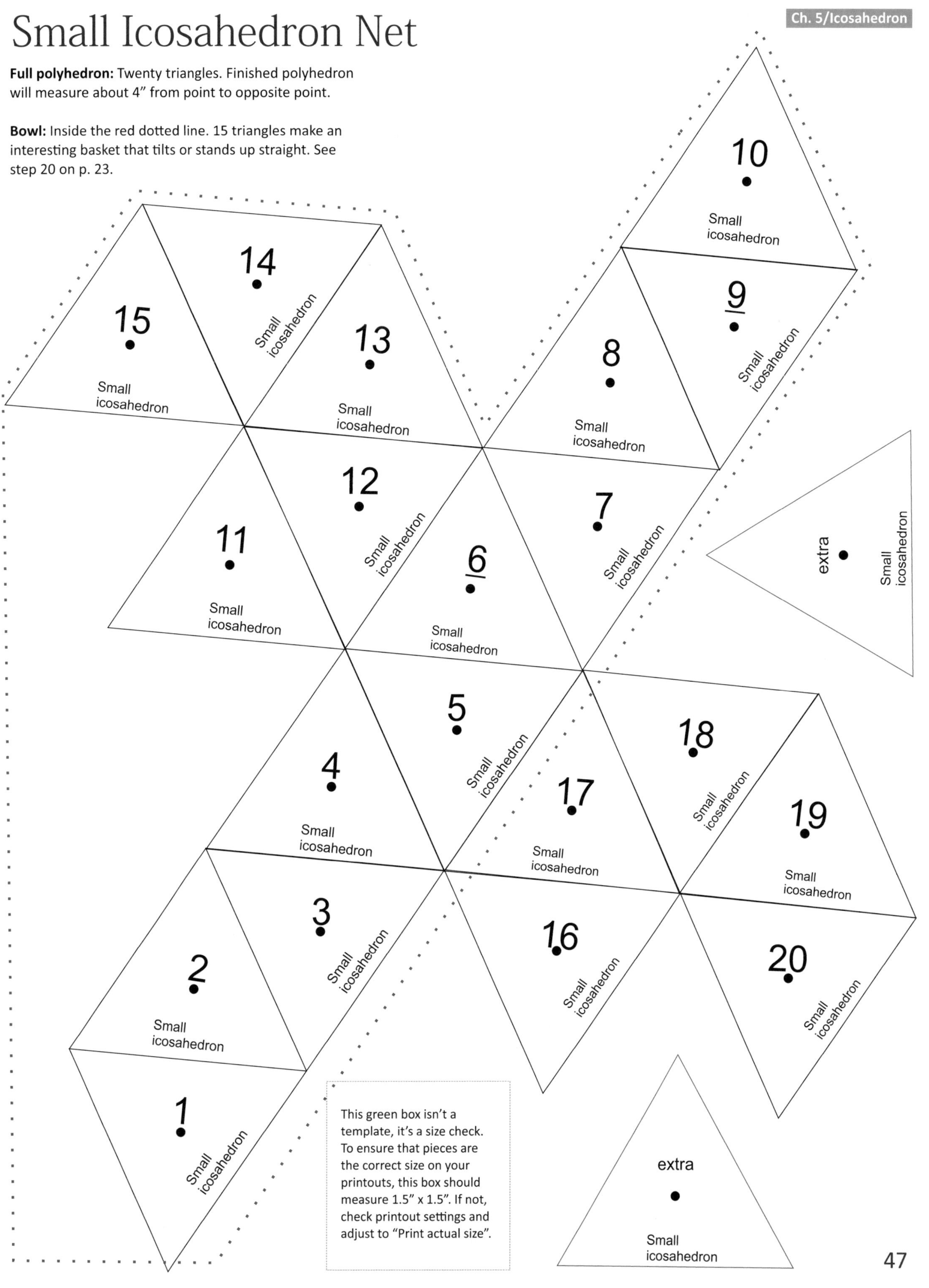

This green box isn't a template, it's a size check. To ensure that pieces are the correct size on your printouts, this box should measure 1.5" x 1.5". If not, check printout settings and adjust to "Print actual size".

Large Icosahedron Templates

Full polyhedron: 20 triangles. This page has only 9, so make 3 copies. This isn't a net – follow the net on the previous page. Will measure about 9" from point to opposite point.
Bowl: 15 triangles. See its net outlined in red on p. 47.

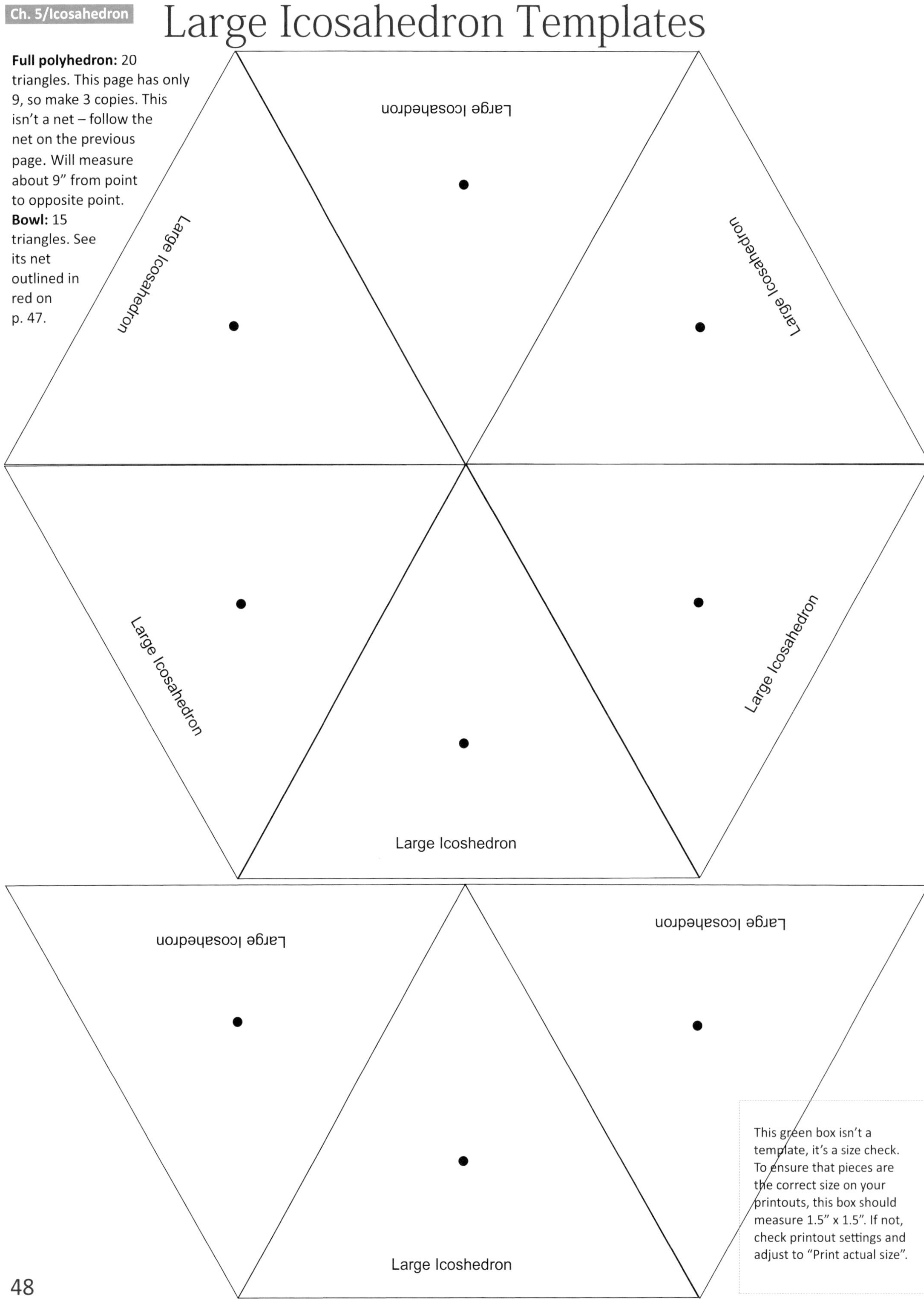

This green box isn't a template, it's a size check. To ensure that pieces are the correct size on your printouts, this box should measure 1.5" x 1.5". If not, check printout settings and adjust to "Print actual size".

Ch. 6/Icosidodecahedron

The small triangles and large number of sides make this a challenge. A full icosidodecadron, like the stuffed toys on the right, has 32 faces. Twelve faces are pentagons, and 20 are triangles. Why work so hard? Because, with contrasting fabrics for the different shapes, 5-pointed-stars shine from it!

The black-and-red ball on the upper right was made from high-contrast prints that fascinate babies. The green-and-white ball was made by Andrea Shlasko, to celebrate bugs!

Project 11 = Jane Austen Dish

> ### Materials
>
> **– Featured fabric** Two strongly contrasting fabrics, small amounts.
>
> **– Lining fabric** Two more contrasting fabrics.
>
> **– Fusible Interfacing**
>
> **– Cardstock**
>
> See also supplies on p. 3.

Above are two views of the featured inside of the bowl. This hilarious fabric has torrid passages from Jane Austen books, plus a dark blue bubbly print for the triangles. Its lining (right) will be on the outside of the bowl, so it won't be as visible. It has a vintage cartoon print and a solid light blue triangles. I used the large templates to create a bowl that measures about 6" across and 3" high.

The featured inside side contains fusible interfacing templates; and the lining/outer side was made using with temporary cardstock templates. I used the whole-project lining method described on p. 12.

1. Photocopy or print out the large net on p. 54 onto cardstock (Except if you're planning to machine-sew the lining – in that case, print the net onto paper.) Cut the shapes apart.

Use a paper/cardstock triangle to cut 10 triangles from fusible interfacing, and a pentagon to cut 6 pentagons from fusible interfacing. (Do this by clipping the template to the interfacing. The technique is explained on p. 5, method 2.)

1

2. Lay each template on the back of the fabric and cut out 1/4" - 1/2" out from all edges. If you want to fussy-cut fabrics for this bowl, see p. 6. For triangles, trim fabric next to and above the template tips to a scant 1/4".

2

continued

3. Follow the procedure in the box on p. 41 to baste the 20 fabric triangles around the triangular fusible interfacing shapes.

Baste the six pentagons as shown on p. 7, method 1. Photo 3 shows all the inside pieces from the back, all basted.

3

4. By hand, sew pieces right sides together (stitches are on p.10), to replicate the half-net on p. 54. Or machine zigzag if you prefer (See p. 11.)

5. After surrounding the central pentagon with star points, add the two additional arm pieces (a pentagon and a triangle).

4

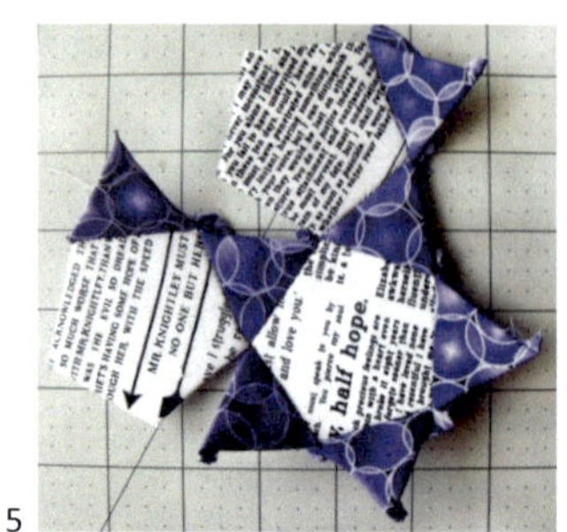
5

6, 7. Stitch up the gaps between the arms, working from the center outwards. Photo 6 shows the finished featured side.

6

7

Assemble the Lining Side

8.Use paper or cardstock templates to cut and baste the lining fabric. Basting methods 1, 2, or 4 on pp. 7-8 are good for this lining, with just a little glue. For the triangles, follow the folding procedure in the box on p. 41, using ironing and glue or starch, instead of interfacing.

Once basted, hand- or machine-stitch the lining pieces into the bowl formation. Some templates may pop out by the time you're done, but that's okay, because you were about to remove them anyway!

9. Remove lining templates! I use a ball-tipped stylus to pry out the edges.

8

9

10. Insert featured side into lining, wrong sides together. Line up the pieces around the rim. Hand-stitch the sides together together around the rim, wrong sides together. See stitch options on p. 10. A traditional whipstitch, ladder stitch, or lacing stitch will work here.

11. I usually start stitching with the featured side pushed down into the inside. But as you progress, the outer lining gets tighter and tighter. When that happens, push the bowl the opposite way, so you're sewing with the lining up.

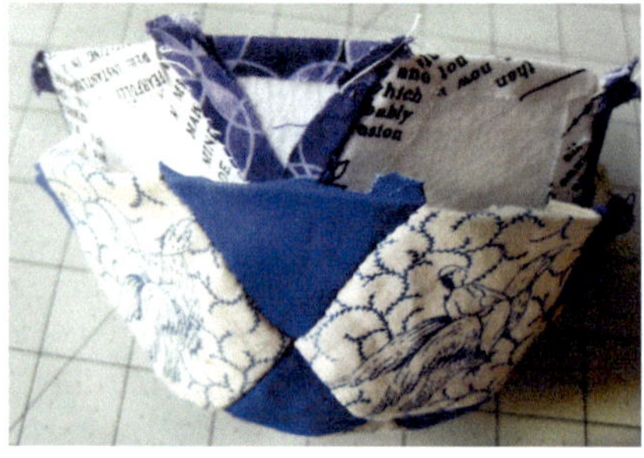
10

12. Finish stitching, then flip the bowl so the featured side is facing up from the inside.

11

12

Project 12 = Coffee-Scented Poinsettia Bowl

This bowl was made from a foil coffee bag, with cardstock templates permanently inside. Each piece is individually lined. That allows you to decide as you go how you would like the rim to look. Every round of additions brings a new contour!

Templates can be cardstock, cardboard, or Kraft-Tex™. With Kraft-Tex™ or interesting cardboard (instead of cardstock) you won't need the third "lining side" (the red plastic in this project).

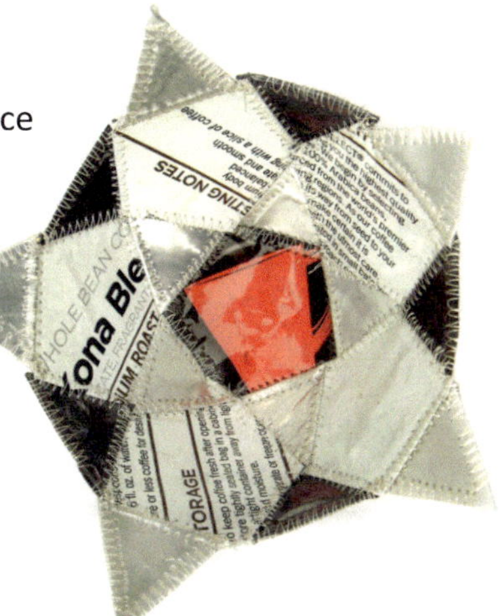

Materials

- **1-2 Coffee bags** Two should be enough to cover all the pieces, front and back.
- **Cardstock, or cardboard** (like from a cereal box), or Kraft Tex™
- **Glue stick**

See also supplies on p. 3

1. Print out small or large templates, pp. 53 or 54, onto cardstock, and cut them apart. (Or: Print on paper and use one of each shape to cut the shapes from cardboard or Kraft-tex™.)

Start with the central pentagon. Place it on a coffee bag, and cut about 1/4" - 1/2" larger all the way around.

2. Temporarily finger press each edge inward and crease.

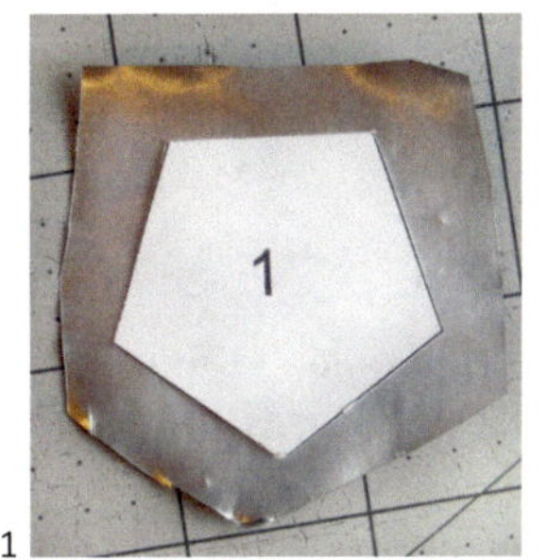

1

2

3. Use another pentagon template to cut any kind of foil or plastic packaging the same size as the template, to cover the back. (I didn't have enough coffee bags – so I used a red plastic bag. If you're using Kraft-Tex™ or cardboard, you may not want or need this additional layer.)

3

4. Place the backing behind the template, in the central piece. Apply a little glue from a stick to hold the layers temporarily.

5. Fold the edges inward again. A little more glue will hold them in place for now, but soon they'll be stitched, so don't worry if they don't stay down well.

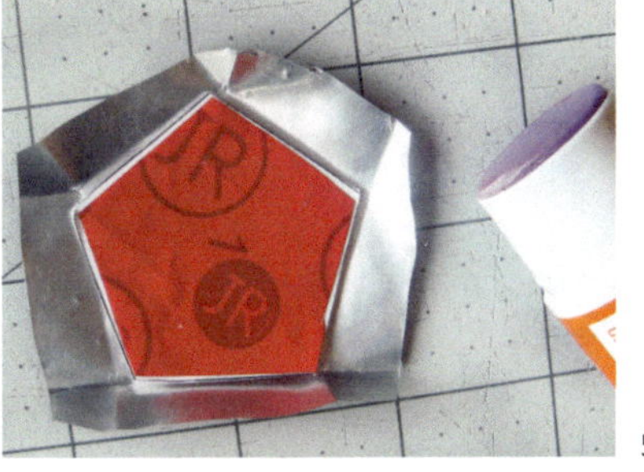
4

5

6. Here's the front of my central piece.

continued

6

Poinsettia bowl, continued

7. Place the triangle templates on the coffee bag, and cut out the bag about 1/4” from the triangle’s edges. You can also trim off the points.

8. Fold inward, so all the folds point in the same direction (Step-by-step triangle basting is in the box on p. 41.) I used the silver inside of the coffee bag as the featured outside, to give the central star silver points.

7

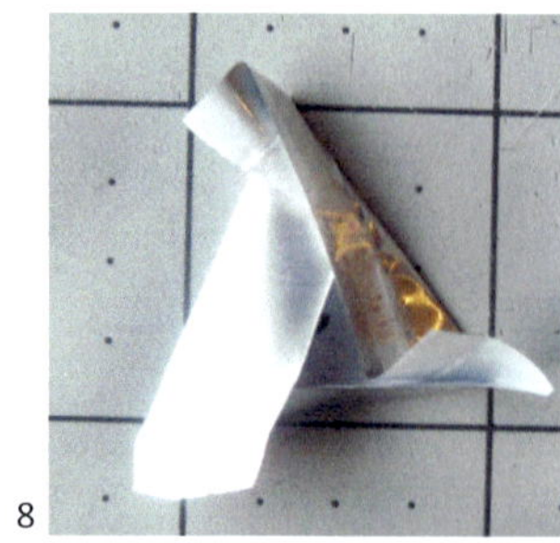
8

If from the back you can’t see the template inside the small triangles, you don’t need an extra lining piece there. If you **can** see the inside of the template, but don’t want to, you can slip a same-size piece to cover the inside of the center back.

9. Load machine with decorative or invisible thread. I used silver metallic thread. With an open-toe appliqué foot for maximum visibility, and a wide zigzag, stitch the silver star points all the way around the central pentagon. Machine stitching tips are on p. 11.

9

10. End of round one: A finished star! (Wouldn’t this make a nice coffee-scented brooch? That’s a weird idea? Never mind!)

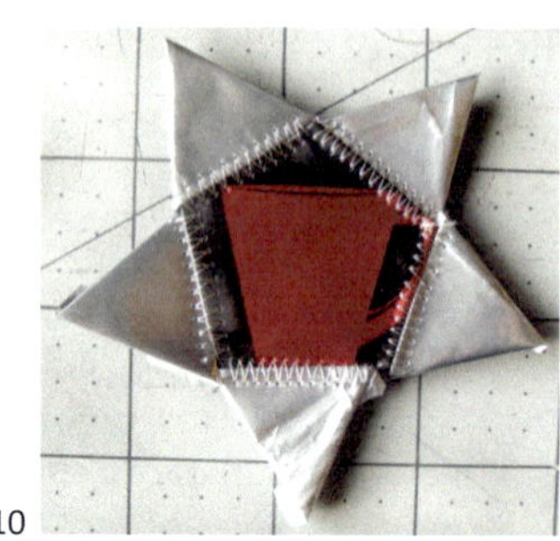
10

11. The next round is pentagons, Prepare five. I used the white bag exterior to contrast against the silver points. When I was done stitching this round, I could have stopped, for the flower petal look in photo 11.

11

12. But I was curious to see what would happen next, so I added brown triangle pieces, to complete the half. Cute! That would have been a good stopping point too!

12

13. But no, I wanted to investigate more! I stitched triangles to the top edge of the pentagons. When pointed up, the bowl looks toothy.

13

14

14, 15. Folding those points outward made it look like a poinsettia! And that’s where I stopped. It’s accidental upcycled Christmas decor!

15

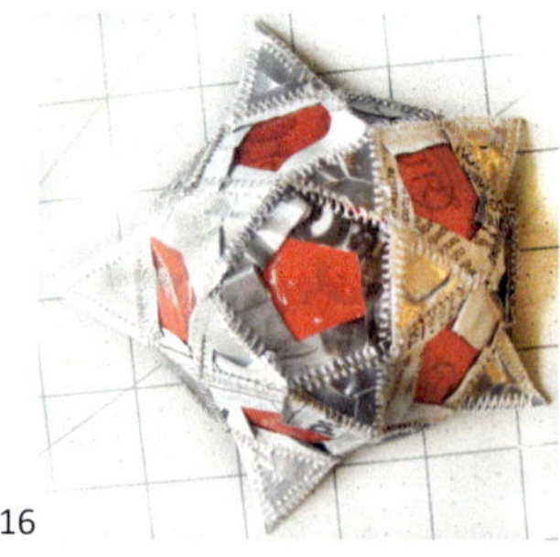
16

Small Icosidodecahedron Net

This size is almost too small to piece in fabric. I suggest you use it only for your paper mockup and/or for recyclables like the coffee bag bowl on p. 51. The large templates on p. 54 are better for fabric and thick interfacing.

Full polyhedron: 32 faces: 12 pentagons and 20 triangles. Create the units on both sides of the red dotted line. Stitch the units together between piece 11 and piece 30. The small size templates will make a 3" polyhedron.

Bowl: Make a small bowl with pieces 1-11; or a fuller bowl with 1-16; or a jagged bowl with 1-16 plus five additional triangles.

This green box isn't a template, it's a size check. To ensure that pieces are the correct size on your printouts, this box should measure 1.5" x 1.5". If not, check printout settings and adjust to "Print actual size".

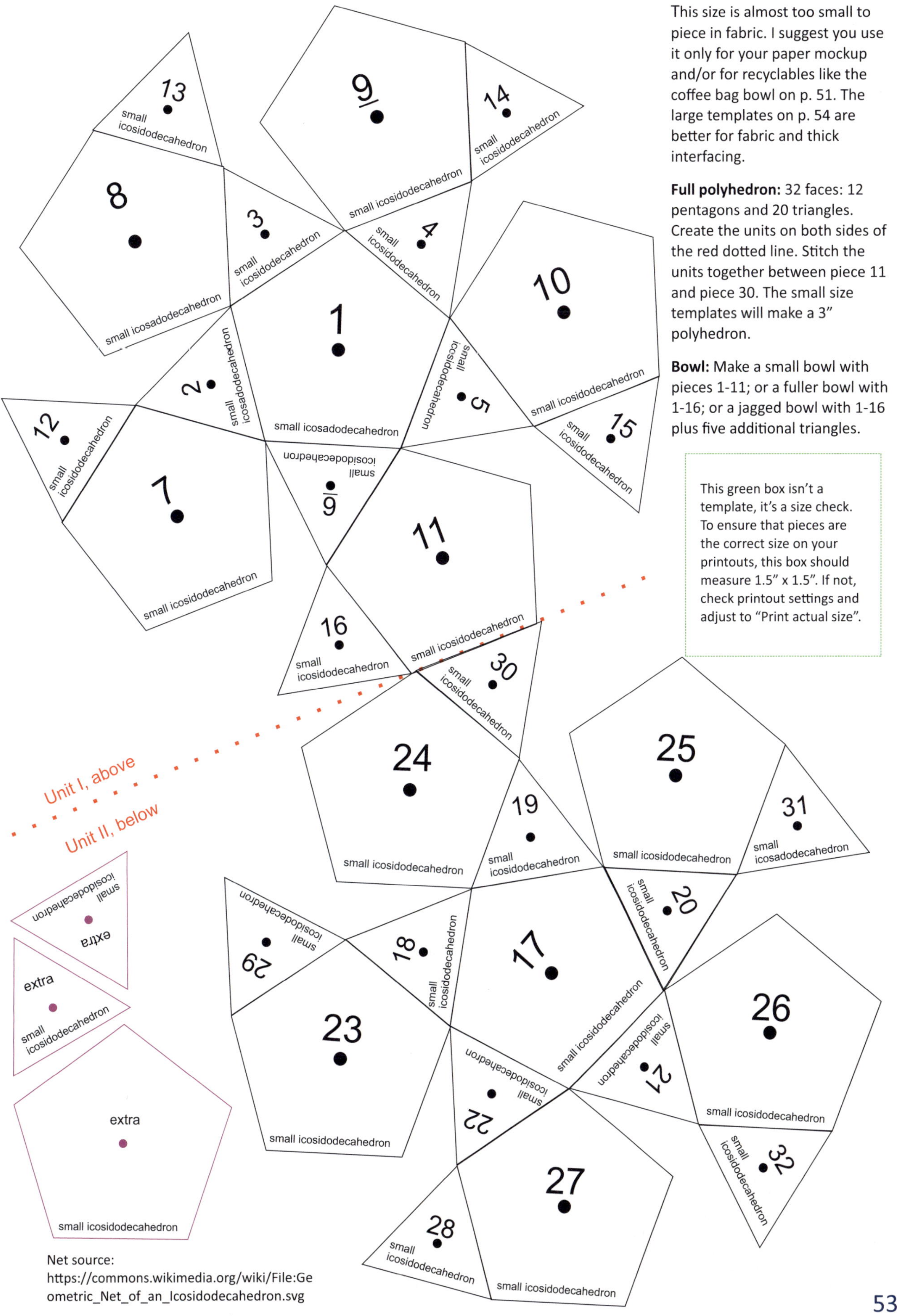

Net source: https://commons.wikimedia.org/wiki/File:Geometric_Net_of_an_Icosidodecahedron.svg

Large Icosidodecahedron Net

Full polyhedron: 32 faces. 12 pentagons and 20 triangles. Make two copies of this page and attach them following the net on the previous page. Large size finishes at about 5" across.

Bowls: Make a small bowl with pieces 1-11; a fuller bowl with 1-16; or a jagged bowl with 1-16 plus five additional triangles.

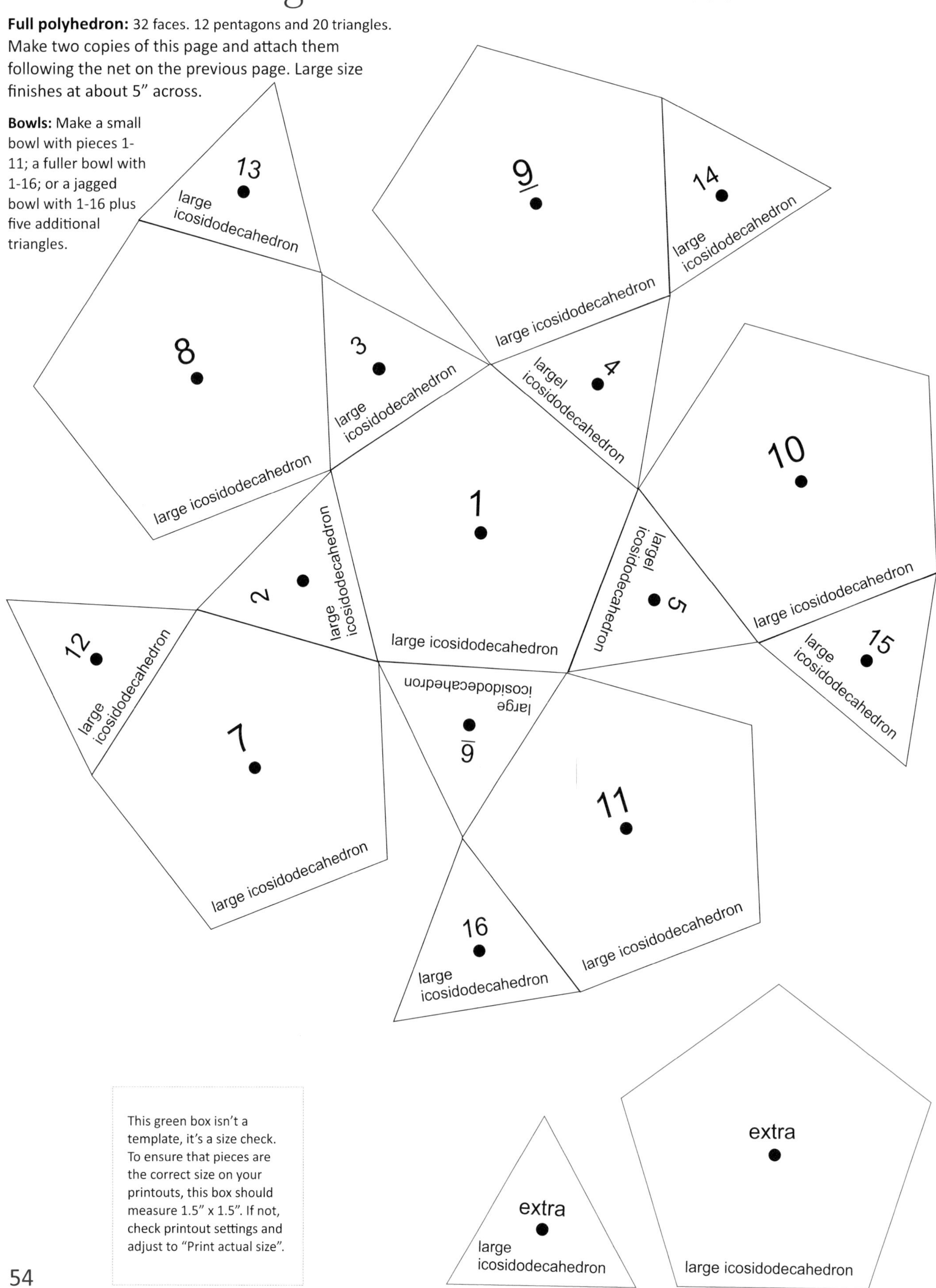

This green box isn't a template, it's a size check. To ensure that pieces are the correct size on your printouts, this box should measure 1.5" x 1.5". If not, check printout settings and adjust to "Print actual size".

Ch. 7/Truncated Icosahedron

The celebrity of the polyhedron world! Most of the world's 6-year-olds recognize this as a soccer ball. Helen Blumen celebrated soccer with her ball on the upper right; my tribute is below.

It's a challenge. The full polyhedron has 32 faces. Twenty are hexagons, and 12 are pentagons. But only 6 pieces are needed for the pink beaded brooch/barrette for a soccer fan, far right. Twenty-three pieces went into the soccer basket below, with an open window handle. It's perfect for a coach or player's bedside table! It can hold everything from an orthodontic retainer to a wedding ring!

Above, soccer ball by Helen Blumen Left, domino ball by the author. Below, beaded silk brooch by the author.

Project 13 = Soccer Bowl

This soccer ball fabric is 20 years old, but I predict you'll find something just as good! Helen Blumen used a much newer mustard-and-black print, upper right. Call your local quilt shop or search online for "soccer quilting fabric".

Even without a soccer print, if you use contrasting fabrics for the hexagons and pentagons, this bowl will scream "soccer!" (at least to soccer fans).

The outer pieces are backed with stiff fusible interfacing. The insides were made with temporary cardstock templates. These directions are for a whole-project lining. but the other lining approaches on pp. 12-13 work, too.

The basket, like the complete large polyhedron, will finish at about 6" at the widest.

Two views of a soccer basket, above and below.

Materials

– **Outside fabric** Two contrasting fabrics, 1 for pentagons (red-and-white polka dot), and 1 for hexagons (soccer balls on blue) in the "large" size templates.

– **Inside fabric** Two contrasting fabrics (here, a gold stripe and a colorful zigzag)

– **Stiff fusible interfacing** For templates behind the outer bowl side

– **Cardstock or paper** For temporary templates behind the inner side.

See also the supplies on p. 3

It's a good idea to make a paper model first. Use the net on bottom of p. 56 for the same configuration as the bowl. Make notes on your model where to place different fabrics.

1. Print the large templates on pages 59 and 60 onto *paper* (if your inner side will be machine stitched) or *cardstock* (if the inside will be hand stitched). I hand stitched my entire project with traditional whipstitches (p. 10).

2. Cut apart the paper or cardboard templates. Clip one of each shape to fusible interfacing, and cut out as many interfacing templates as you need (with my plan, 7 pentagons and 16 hexagons).

3. Starting with the ball fabric/outer side: At the ironing board, place the fusible interfacing templates, one by one, on the soccer fabric. Use one of the fussy cut techniques on p. 6 to center motifs. Cut the fabric 1/2" larger than the template, and fuse the fabric around the template, as described on pp. 7-8.

4, 5. When you have several fuse-basted pentagons and hexagons, start recreating the net on p. 56. Compared to the full polyhedron, I left out pieces on one side, added more to another, and made a window (circled in photo 5), by leaving out the pentagon that was supposed to go in the middle.

continued

4

5

Use cardstock or paper templates to baste the same number of pieces – 7 pentagons and 16 hexagons – for the inside of this bowl.

6, 7. This project is asymmetrical, so the inside must MIRROR the outer "lining". Set printer for a mirror image of the net below. Or, use my hands-on approach: I placed the soccer ball exterior in front of me, unfinished side out. Then I placed the striped lining pieces onto it, wrong side down. On by one, I positioned each piece, pulled it off and stitched it permanently in position. Then I put the growing lining BACK on top of the featured side, and positioned the next piece. I kept going like this, to ensure I was matching and mirroring the ball print side.

8. It's VERY easy to lose one's bearings. So I established a landmark. It's the red piece circled in photo 8, the lowest pentagon on the bowl's rim. It's also marked with a red star in piece 21 on the net below. On the lining side, I placed a giant fluorescent green paper clip to mark the corresponding pentagon (it's circled.)

9. The last step is stitching the rims and circumference of the window together. It must be stitched with the non-interfaced side on the inside, wrong sides together. Photo 9 shows a side view of the finished basket (with the landmark circled.) A traditional whipstitch, ladder stitch, or lacing stitch work well here.

6

7

8

9

Asymmetric Soccer Bowl Net

There are 7 pentagons and 16 hexagons. Use the large templates on pp. 58-59 (this net is too small). You'll need 2 copies of p. 59 and 1 copy of p. 60. Don't sew anything to the orange edges – those are rim or window edges. The red star shows a natural landmark, the lowest pentagon on the rim. Paper clip or safety pin it on your fabric versions. Print this net out as your guide for making the outside; print a mirror image to serve as a map/net for the inside.

Project 14 = Soccer Flower Brooch

This quick project is about 3.5" across. I stitched a brooch pin on back, but you could also sew it to a hair clip, elastic, headband, or hat. It's the perfect accessory for a young soccer player or coach! The project is machine stitched and hand-embellished.

Materials

– **Featured and backing fabric** I used pink dupioni silk for the petals, gold dupioni for the center pentagon, and purple on back.
– **Pin backing** or other finding
– **Beads**
– **Stiff fusible interfacing** Double-sided is best here. If you only have 1-sided, rub a glue stick on the other side.
– **Cardstock or paper**
– **Decorative machine thread**
– See also supplies on p. 3

1. Print the small net on p. 58 onto paper or cardstock. Cut out pieces 1-6 as a single unit.

2. Clip the paper shape to stiff fusible interfacing, and cut the interfacing to the same size.

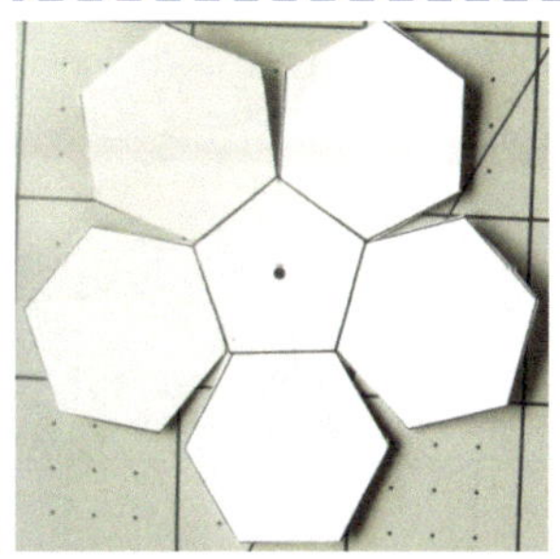
1

2

3. Fuse fabric to the back.

4. Cut the backing even with the interfacing.

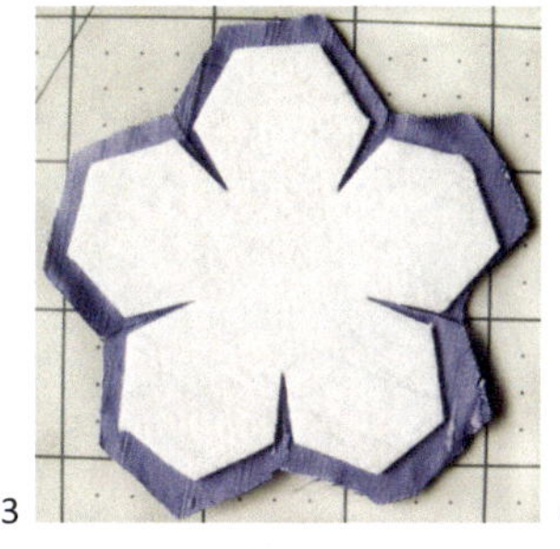
3

4

5. Flip the piece to the featured fabric and fuse rough-cut fabric in place. Trim the featured fabric to the same size as the interfacing.

6. Cut apart your paper or cardstock net. Use a paper pentagon to cut a pentagon from contrasting fabric (I chose gold). Use a glue stick (or fusible web) to place the pentagon in the center.

5

6

7. When the glue dries, with decorative thread on top, and invisible or back-matching thread on bottom, satin stitch the pentagon down. I chose gold thread on top and invisible thread in the bobbin.

8. Freemotion quilt 3 or 4 contour lines up center of each petal. Satin stitch each dart outward, pushing the edges together as you sew (see p. 11). I used orange thread.

7

8

9. Satin stitch all the way around the rim. I continued using the orange thread, with invisible thread in the bobbin. Hand-sew beads as desired.

10. Sew or glue a pin or hair finding to the back. If you must stitch it on, make sure the stitches don't penetrate to the front.

9

10

Small Truncated Icosahedron Net

Full Polyhedron: 32 faces. 12 are pentagons (grey), and 20 are hexagons (white.) If #1 is its base, #32 will be the roof. In this small size, the polyhedron will be about 3" across.

Bowl or **Brooch:** A flower brooch or shallow bowl is inside the red dotted line.

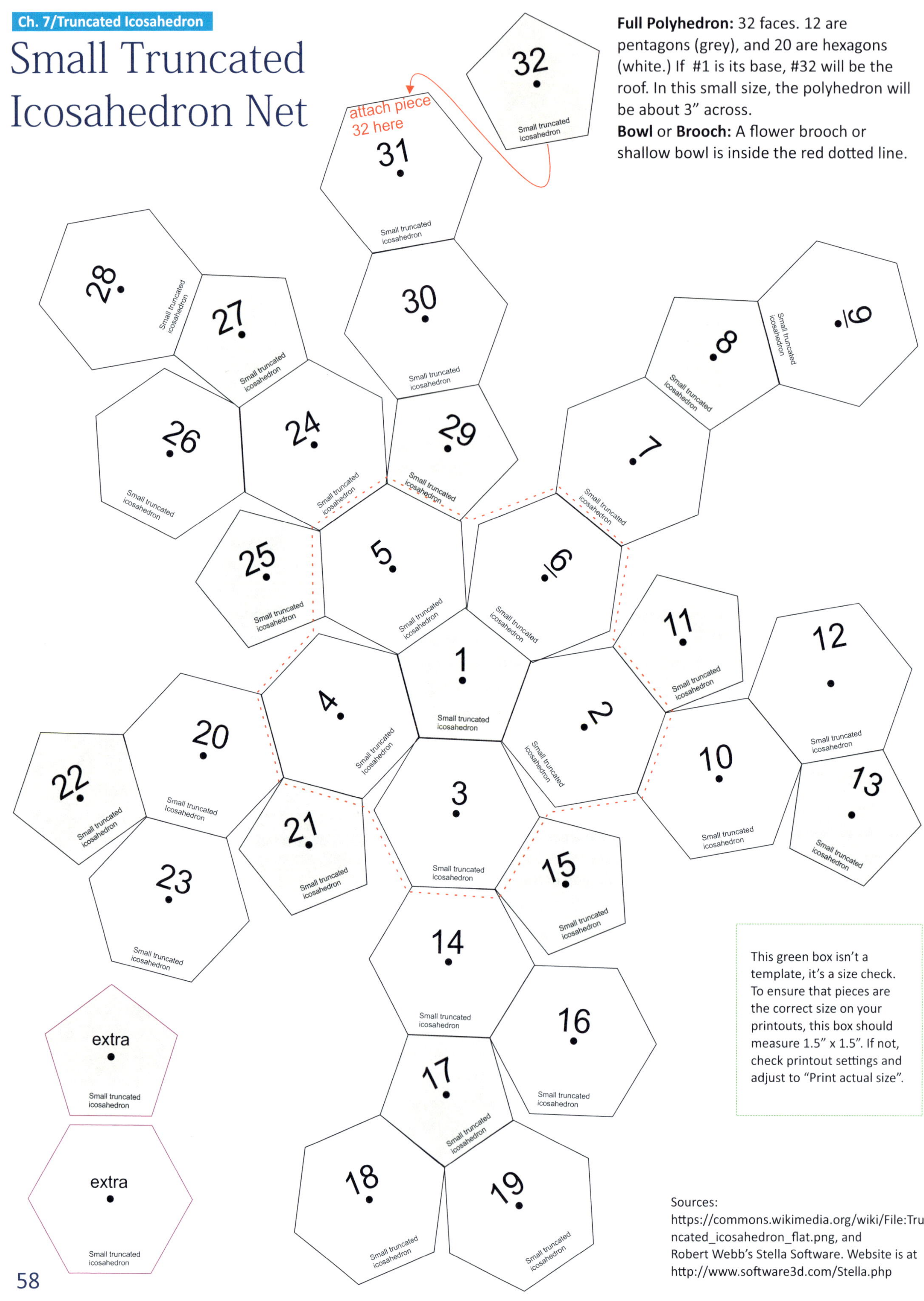

This green box isn't a template, it's a size check. To ensure that pieces are the correct size on your printouts, this box should measure 1.5" x 1.5". If not, check printout settings and adjust to "Print actual size".

Sources: https://commons.wikimedia.org/wiki/File:Truncated_icosahedron_flat.png, and Robert Webb's Stella Software. Website is at http://www.software3d.com/Stella.php

Large Truncated Icosahedron Hexagon Templates

There are 13 hexagons on this page. The soccer bowl on p. 55 requires all 16; a complete polyhedron requires 20, so print out two copies of this page for either. You'll also need the pentagons on the next page. Note: This is not a net. Use the net arrangement on p. 58.

Full Polyhedron: 32 faces. 12 are pentagons, 20 are triangles. It will measure about 6" across.

Shallow Bowl or Brooch: See red outlined area on p. 58.

This green box isn't a template, it's a size check. To ensure that pieces are the correct size on your printouts, this box should measure 1.5" x 1.5". If not, check printout settings and adjust to "Print actual size".

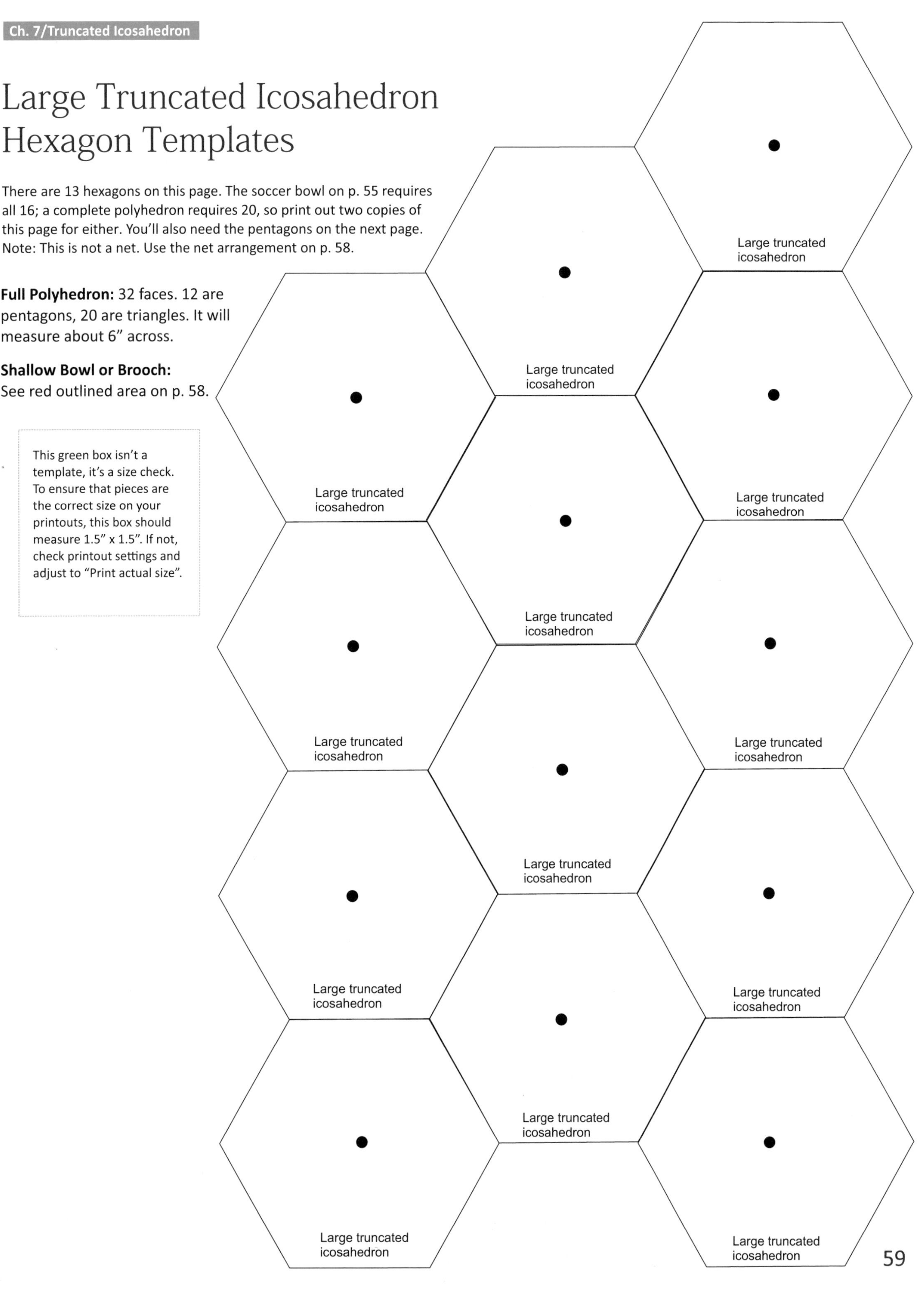

Large Truncated Icosahedron Pentagon Templates

Here are 13 pentagon templates, enough to make one complete polyhedron, plus an extra. Combine them with 20 of the hexagon templates printed on the previous page. Note: This is not a net. For construction, follow the net arrangement on p. 58.

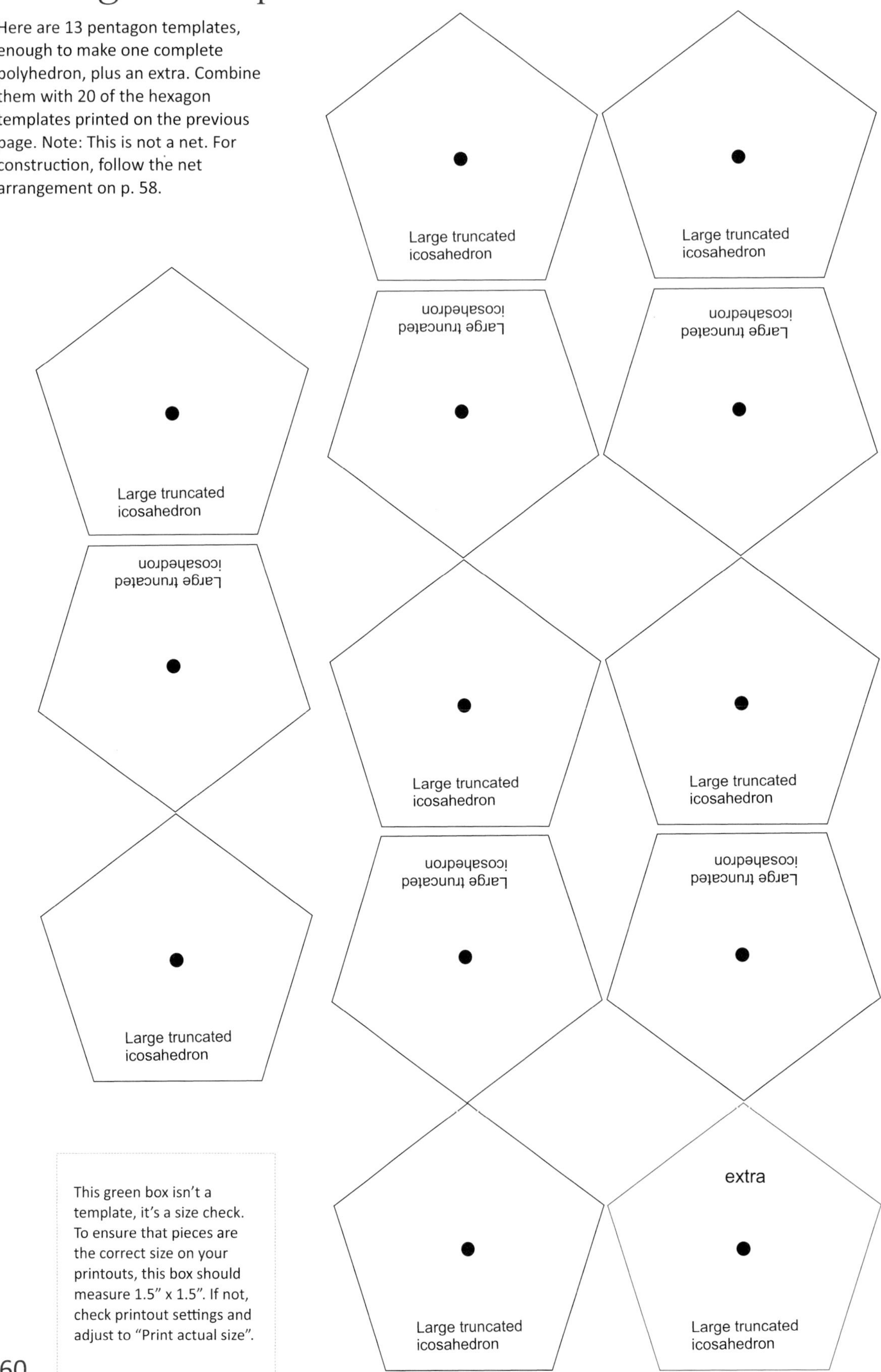

This green box isn't a template, it's a size check. To ensure that pieces are the correct size on your printouts, this box should measure 1.5" x 1.5". If not, check printout settings and adjust to "Print actual size".

Ch. 8/Stellated Dodecahedron

If you made a dodecahdron – even just a paper model – you are qualified to make a regal stellated dodecadron. This challenging project must be handsewn.

What's the connection between the simple shape in Ch. 2 and these complex angular shapes? The base. Each star point – "stellation" – has five triangular sides. Their base forms a pentagon, and the pentagons are arranged like a dodecahedron.

Just as a regular dodecahdron has 12 faces, this polyhedron has 12 stellations. Multiply 12 by the 5 triangular faces, for a total of 60 faces. But I'm not emotionally prepared to cut and sew 60 triangles! So we'll take a huge shortcut: Folds will distinguish the faces, not separate pieces of fabric. You can use up to 12 different fabrics per stellated dodecahedron, not 60.

For the polka-dot batik star on the far right above (and below), I removed the cardstock templates as a last step before stuffing. That makes the shape plump.

For the black-white-and-red polyhedron in the middle above (and that little Abe is attempting to conquer on the right), and the rainbow batik polyhedron on the left, I figured out a way to put sharp creases into fusible interfacing, which shows off the flat faces. Project 16 explains how.

If you want a stellated dodecahedron that's PURELY ornamental – it will never be played with, munched upon (as my grandson was longing to do), or sat upon – you can use scored and folded cardstock instead of fusible interfacing inside.

Using the small size template will result in a star approximately 6" from point to opposite point. With large templates, that measurement will be about 8".

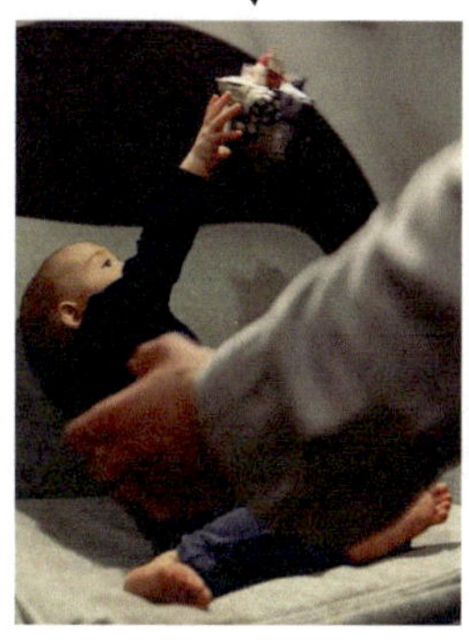

Action shot of my grandbaby attempting to grab a stellated dodecahedron mobile, as his parent rushes to intervene! See the first photo in this series on p. 1.

Materials

- **Featured fabric** Small amounts of up to 12 fabrics, for each stellation to be different. For the one in the photo, I started with a precut roll of multicolored 2.5" batik strips.
- **Cardstock**
- **School glue stick** .
- **Polyester stuffing**
- **Ball tip stylus or other tool for scoring (indenting) paper**

See also the supplies on p. 3

Project 15 = Chubby Baby Star

The small dodecahedron net on p. 20 will also serve as the net for this project. Refer to it during this process, but there's no need to print or cut out its individual pieces....

...Unless you want to closely control which piece is placed next to which. In that case, print p. 20 onto paper and cut out the entire net (not the individual shapes); then fold and tape it into a model. Write the color or fabric you want to use on each face. Then cut the tape and flatten the net again – that will be your stellation cone placement map!

continued

Chubby star, continued

1. Whether you chose small (p. 70) or large (p. 71), you'll need to print two copies onto cardstock. Use a ruler and scoring tool (see p. 3 for options) to firmly indent all the way across all the lines inside each "umbrella," **except** the red dotted line – that's a cutting line.

2, 3. Cut out the umbrellas, then cut them in half along the red dotted lines. You need 12 half-umbrellas.

4. Bend paper forward along scored lines.

5. Use templates to cut fabrics, about 1/2" bigger, all the way around.

6. The green arrows show where the internal lines meet the cardstock's top edge. These are crucial landmarks.

7. Turn the lower right vertical edge inward, against the cardstock. A glue stick helps. Press with a finger, or better, an iron.

8, 9. Press inward the seam allowance along the second triangle up from the bottom right. This creates a small pleat. Use glue if needed to press that pleat flat. (Avoid getting lots of glue on templates, because they'll come out.)

10, 11. Press. Continue like this. The beginning of each pleat should be exactly where the triangle lines meet the top cardstock edge. (Where the pleat lands lower down doesn't matter.)

12. When you reach the lower left corner, press up the bottom edge on the left.

13. Fold in the raw left edge at that same corner to the right, so the seam allowance flap extends downward.

14. On the opposite edge – at the bottom far right corner – press the seam allowance upwards (circled).

continued

15. Dab a bit of glue inside the bottom flap, even if you're planning to remove the cardstock before finishing. It will help prevent the template from popping out prematurely. **Glue a little to the right and left but not in the exact center.**

15

16. Thread a slender needle with strong thread that matches the fabric. Begin by putting a knot toward the end of your thread and bringing the needle up through the center back. Pull to the knot and take an extra tiny stitch in the seam allowance.

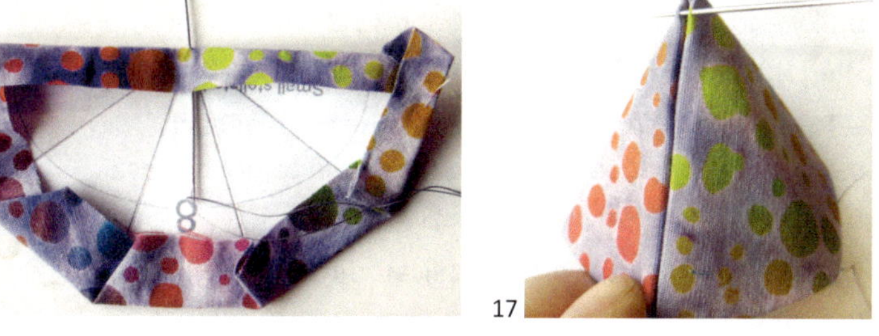
16 17

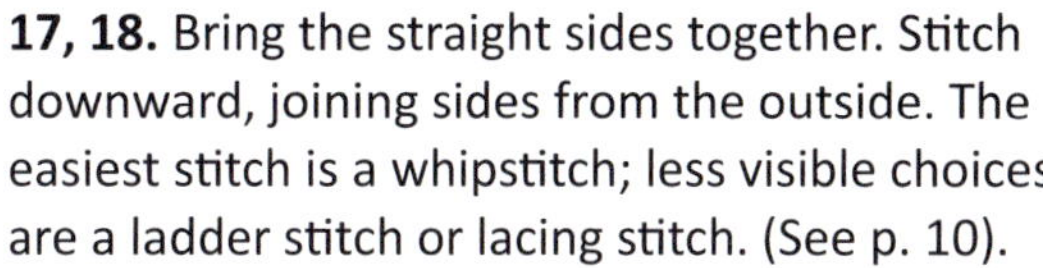

17, 18. Bring the straight sides together. Stitch downward, joining sides from the outside. The easiest stitch is a whipstitch; less visible choices are a ladder stitch or lacing stitch. (See p. 10).

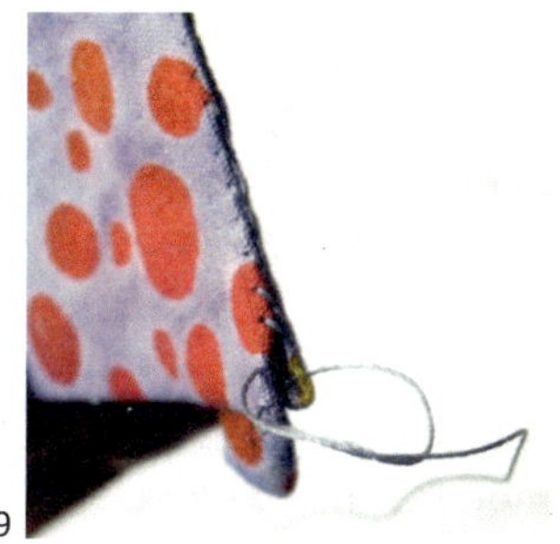

19. At the bottom, do a loop knot (p. 9)

18 19

20. Bring the needle through the seam at the bottom, pull it out on the other side, and do 2-3 tiny stitches in the seam allowance on the back, followed by a loop knot. Cut thread.

20

21

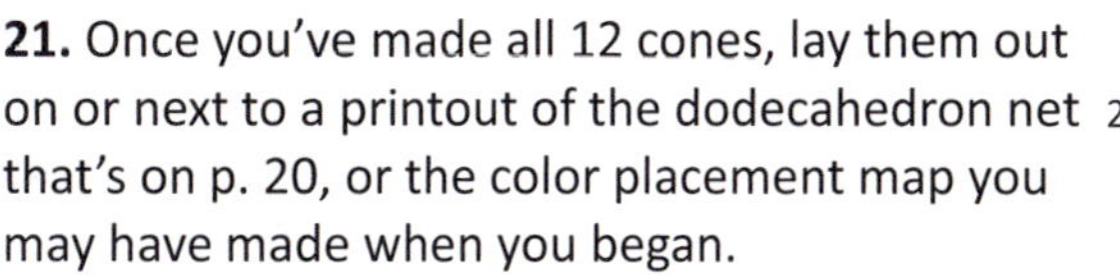

21. Once you've made all 12 cones, lay them out on or next to a printout of the dodecahedron net that's on p. 20, or the color placement map you may have made when you began.

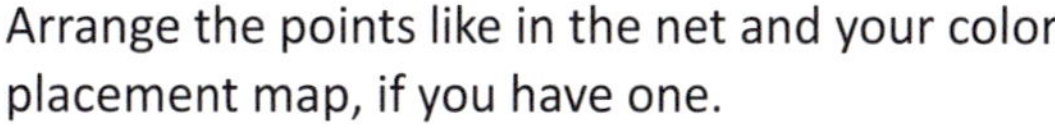

Arrange the points like in the net and your color placement map, if you have one.

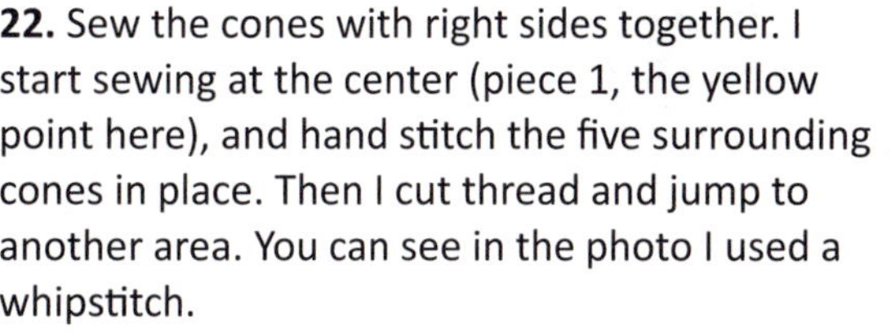

22. Sew the cones with right sides together. I start sewing at the center (piece 1, the yellow point here), and hand stitch the five surrounding cones in place. Then I cut thread and jump to another area. You can see in the photo I used a whipstitch.

22

continued

Chubby star, continued

As you sew keep the following in mind:

– You are sewing from vertex to vertex. The beginning of each pleat, and the tiny cardstock point underneath, marks each vertex. I hold the two end vertices together while stitching toward them.

– When you jump from one piece to the next, photo 23, an extra tacking stitch in the corner helps maintain tension.

– Avoid placing the seams of different cones against each other. It will happen occasionally, but avoid it as much as you can, because seams bashing together can become bulky and confusing. Photo 24 shows the ideal – no more than one cone seam per meeting of three points.

– To move the seam allowance at the base of each stellation out of your way, you may have to pry it loose from the glue. A ball-tip stylus can help.

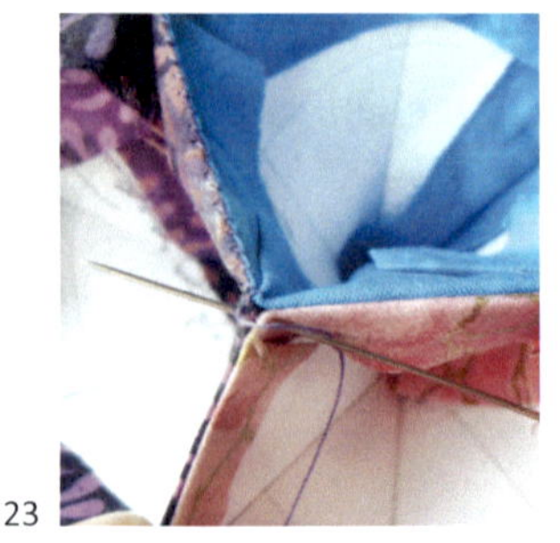

23

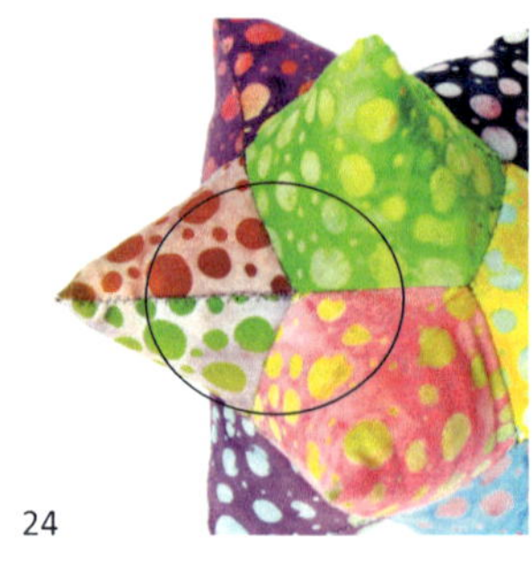

24

25. Add pieces until you've replicated the dodecahedron net on p. 20.

26, 27. Sew the remaining seams that curl up the shape. I start at the central piece, and stitch outward. Fascinating things happen. For example, the five points that meet in photo 26 can be "popped" open – and that purple central point in photo 27 pops up, like a hungry baby bird's beak!

25

26

28. You may realize you've created an abstract sculpture/wearable art. Wouldn't this make a great scarf (with a few hundred more points?)

27

28

29. Things keep tightening. If you didn't glue the cardstock much, some templates might start falling out. Glue them back in if you really need them, but you'll probably be fine without them, because your creases remain to show you where to sew.

30. When it becomes impossible to sew the remaining edges right sides together, pull out all templates and turn everything gently to the right side. Join the remaining edges from the good side. A whipstitch or lacing stitch is easiest here (p. 10).

29

30

31. Leave at least two edges open and fill with polyester stuffing. Use a pencil's eraser end, a ball-tipped stylus, chopsticks, or my favorite stuffing tool, a curved neck hemostat, to push the stuffing up into the points. Pull out any remaining templates, and stitch up the gap with a whipstitch or lacing stitch. You're done! Send pictures!

31

Project 16 = Angular Silk Star

After the previous project, I was faced (pun!) with a challenge: Could I make a chiseled version, to show off all 60 lovely triangular faces?

For my first experiment, I scored cardstock templates, folded the cardstock outward against the fabric, creating sharp faces - and then kept the cardstock inside permanently.

This worked so well that I made two of them. But I knew they weren't sturdy. If someone sat on them, or spilled something under them, or tried to eat one like my grandbaby on p. 61, the cardstock could be irreparably damaged.

I couldn't put a neat crease in fusible interfacing, no matter how much I tried to fold it. I was stuck.

Then, one morning, I woke up and the solution flashed on me: What if I *machine stitched* the lines between faces on the interfacing, using the paper templates as a guide? And it worked! Lines of stitching help the interfacing fold sharply and accurately! So that's what we'll do here, for a durable, playable, and semi-edible ornament.

Materials

- **Featured fabric** If you want each stellation to be different, small amounts of 12 fabrics. I used dupioni silks.
- **Stiff fusible interfacing**
- **Polyester stuffing**

See also supplies on p. 3

Before you start: Take a look at p. 20, the small dodecahedron net. That's the layout for this project.

If you want to arrange fabrics in a specific way, consider printing p. 20 onto paper, and taping it into a model (see p. 4). Write the color or fabric you want on each face. Then flatten the net again, and you have your cone placement map.

Choose template size. The small size on p. 70 will make a 7" high star; the large size, p.71, creates an 8" star. Print two copies of the size you want on paper, not cardstock.

1, 2. Cut out 12 half-umbrellas. Clip each to the fusible side of interfacing. With 2-sided (or interfacing with no fusible), place paper on the rougher side, if there is one. This side will wind up on back.

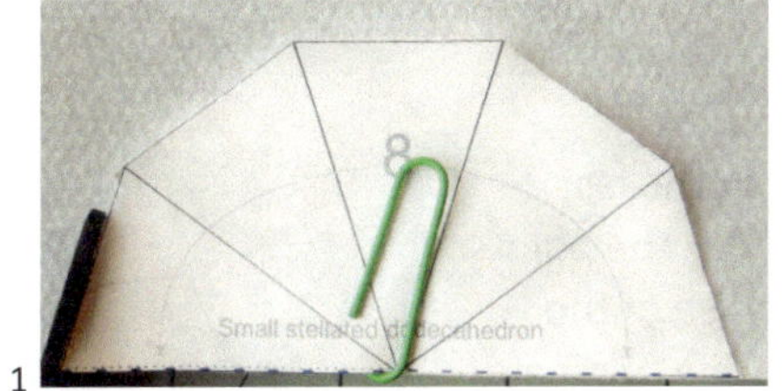

1

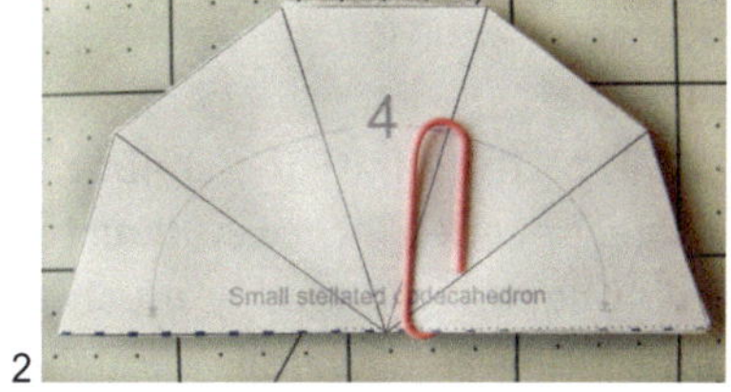

2

3, 4. Set machine to a short straight stitch. Make sure the top thread color strongly contrasts with interfacing (I used navy thread). On the bobbin side – which will go behind the front – use invisible or white thread to hide stitches (if your fabric is see-through).

3

Holding paper and interfacing together (I used a paper clip), straight stitch along the four interior lines. Start at 1, stitching inward to top center; out to 2; clip threads. Stitch inward again at 3; out to 4. Accuracy is important where stitches meet edges.

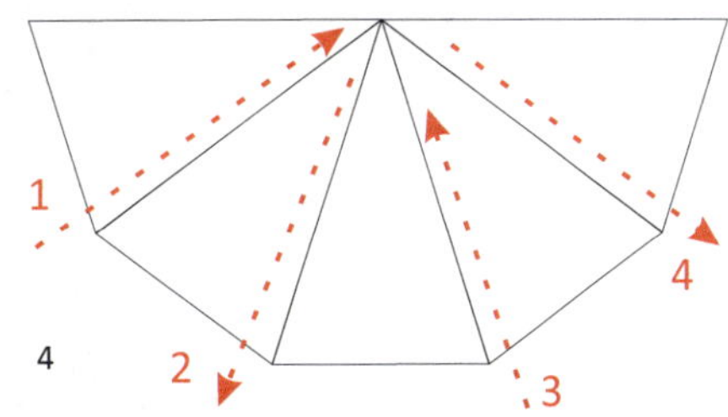

4

5. Wiggle the shape back and forth like a loose tooth, along all the stitching lines, until they fold easily.

5

6. Tear out and discard the five paper triangles from each segment.

6

continued

Angular star, continued

7

8

7. Use interfacing pieces to cut fabric for each stellation, about 1/2" bigger than the template, all the way around.

9

10

8, 9, 10. At the ironing board, press the right seam allowance inward. Then, moving up and around, fold each edge over, creating a pleat each time. *The beginning of the pleat should be exactly where the stitched triangle lines meet the edge of the interfacing.* On p. 62, follow steps 6-14, but here you're fusing the fabric inward.

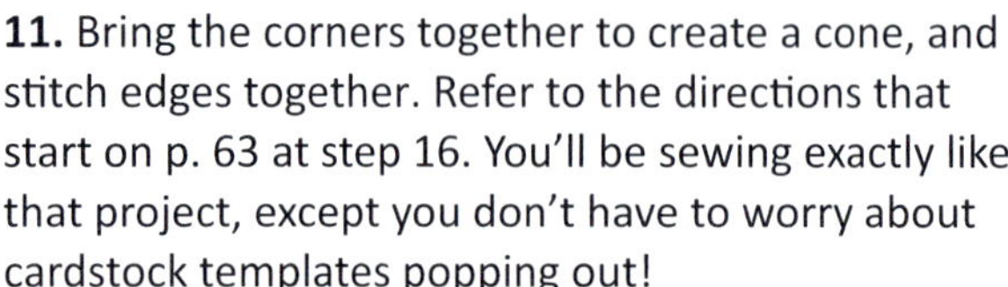

11. Bring the corners together to create a cone, and stitch edges together. Refer to the directions that start on p. 63 at step 16. You'll be sewing exactly like that project, except you don't have to worry about cardstock templates popping out!

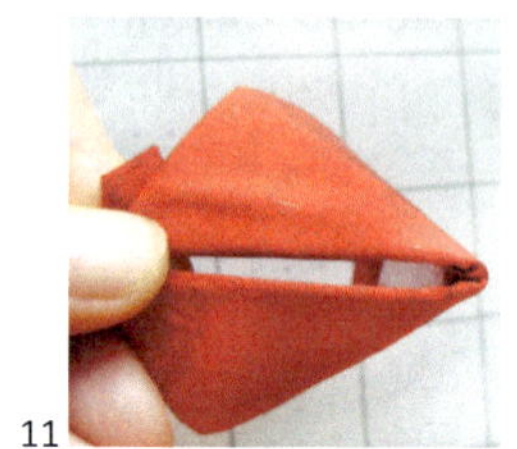
11

Continue following the directions through to the end, on p. 63. The difference: you'll have to turn the form to the outside much sooner.

When working from the outside, the stitching requires maneuvering. If you've been using one of the stitches on p. 10, try a different one – it might be easier for you.

12

12. Time to stuff it! The chubby star in the last project needed lots of stuffing to fill out the points. This one doesn't need as much because of the interfacing. It just needs enough stuffing to create tension that will hold the cones in position.

13. When it's stuffed, sew up the last edges. Pat yourself on the back! Then make a couple more, because I discovered by accident that stellated dodecahedrons stack beautifully!

13

Project 17 = Partially-Stellated Dodecahedr-ish Dishes, Gift Boxes, Doll Yurts, and Beyond!

These toys and ornaments are made from the dodecahedron templates in Ch. 2, plus the corresponding stellation templates in this chapter. They are all hand-sewn, and a superfun challenge.

Top row: Candy wrappers and frozen broccoli packaging went into this half stellated dodecahedron ornament.

Here are 3 views of a unique cave with 9 interior pentagon faces, and three exterior stellations, one of which is a flap. It's a home to a small plastic animals, and can stand in many different positions.

Row 3: Made with small templates, this is a 5" high rocket ship (or yurt or doghouse) with 11 interior pentagons, and 6 exterior stellations. Two of the side petals open out like a Tesla/De Lorean. Also makes a dramatic presentation box for a small gift.

After making several complete stellated dodecahedra, I wondered: Is it possible to add just a few stellation cones to a bowl?

There was one big problem: Stellations, whether cardstock or interfacing - are a mess inside. On the right you see a bunch of them halfway through a stellated dodecahedron.

Then it occurred to me: Maybe I could stitch a pentagon into each opening, to block the messy view!

continued

Put mathematically – hah! Just kidding, I can't do math! But I did come up with a formula. It goes like this:

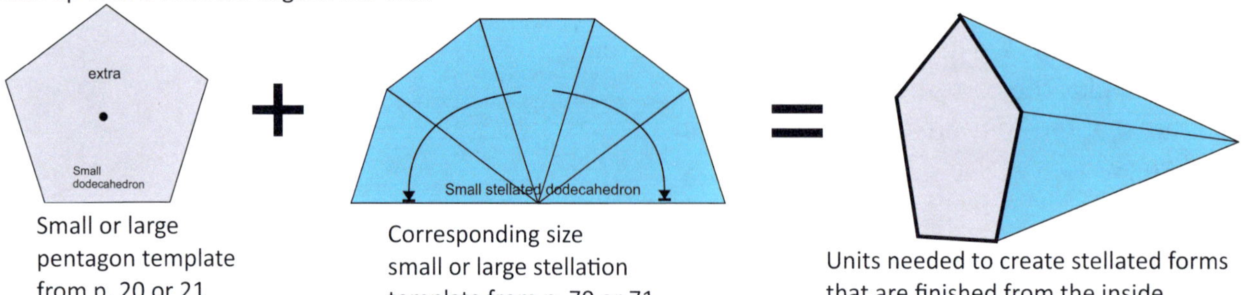

Small or large pentagon template from p. 20 or 21

Corresponding size small or large stellation template from p. 70 or 71

Units needed to create stellated forms that are finished from the inside

Thus stellation cones became building block units. Want to make your own yurt with these units? Here goes!

1. Make a cardstock model, first, to explore creative options. Print out pentagon and stellation templates – large or small size. The pages are noted in the diagram, above. Cut and tape your way to a paper model. My yurt prototype – cut from a variety of cardstock scraps – is shown at right. I taped five stellations around a flat base pentagon, plus one more stellation on top.

1

2. Print the size template you want on cardstock: the small or large pentagon templates on p. 20 or 21, and corresponding size small or large stellation templates on p. 70 or 71.

Use one of each cardstock shape to cut six stellation templates and six pentagon templates from fusible interfacing.

Cover one side of the interfacing cone templates with fabric. Directions start on p. 65, steps 1-11 (it will also refer you to p. 62-3, steps 1-19.)

2

3. Baste fabric over one side of six fusible interfacing pentagons, following the procedure on p. 8, method 3.

3

4. Stitching the 6 pentagons into the 6 cone opening is tricky. The ladder stitch on p. 10 is the least visible. You don't want these stitches to show much because there will be more stitching on top of them to join pieces. It must be done by hand.

5. The other units needed are five more pentagons that are flat and finished on both sides (six if you want to "shut" the front door).

4

5

6. To make those, cut five more small or large pentagon templates from interfacing, and baste the featured side fabric to them. To create the reverse side, I made individual turned edge linings, explained on p. 13. In photo 6, the interfaced side is on the left, and its reverse side is on the far right, ready to be stitched in place. Stitch them wrong sides together, any way you like, from the choices on p. 13.

6

continued

Now you have 5-6 flat pentagons finished on both sides, and 6 stellation units. Arrange them using the annotated net on the bottom of this page. (It's the same as the net on p. 20, but with information about stellation placement.)

8, 9. Here are pieces 1-6 joined. Photo 9 shows the underside.

10, 11. As it grew, it started to look like a sci-fi dune crawler.

8 9

12. Stitch up the sides. I left the sides of the longest arm – made up of pieces 6-12 in the net below – unstitched, so it could open and shut like a DeLorean. I initially left the seam between pieces 5/10 and 4/9 unsewn so they could open too, below. (Eventually I sewed up that seam.) Fun!

10 11

12

Yurt net

Use this for reference. It's almost the same as the dodecahedron net, but this size is too small to make in fabric. It shows the placement of flat and stellated units. Use the small or large pentagon templates on pp. 20 or 21, along with the small or large stellation templates on pp. 70 or 71.

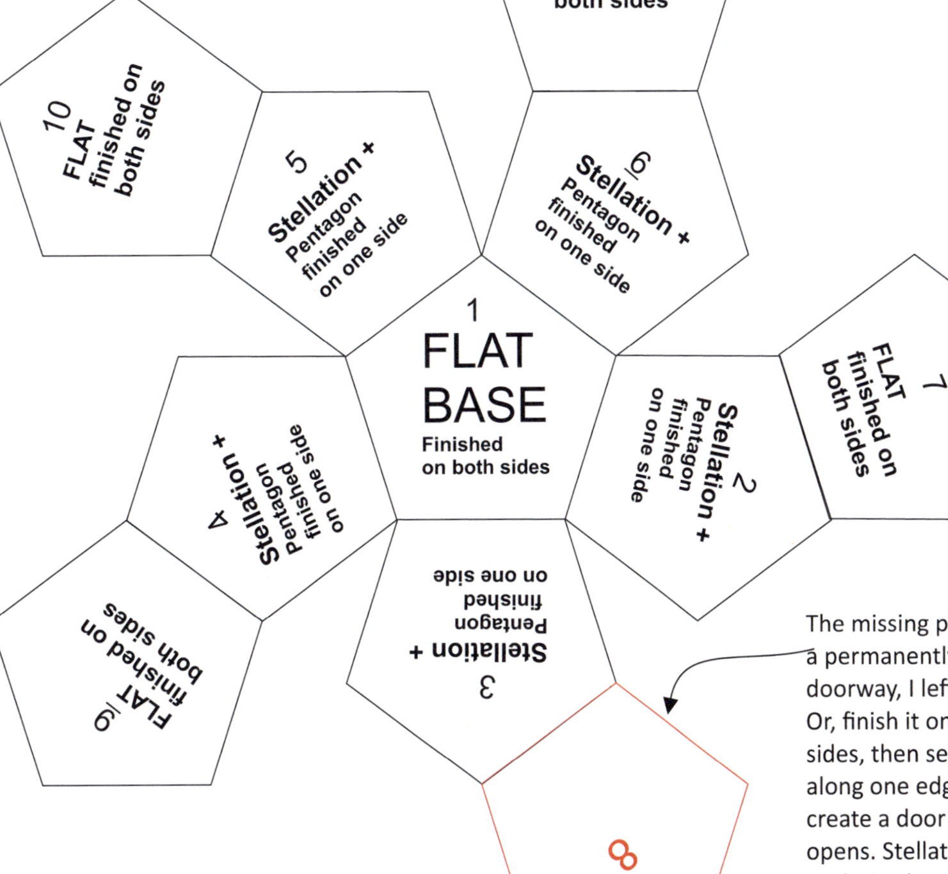

The missing piece. For a permanently open doorway, I left it off. Or, finish it on both sides, then sew it only along one edge to create a door that opens. Stellate or not, as desired.

Small Stellated Dodecahedron Templates

Full polyhedron Requires 12 half "umbrellas". Will measure about 7" from point to opposite point. Print out 2 copies of this page. On the second copy, cross out the numbers and add numbers 10-12. There will be 6 extra.

Score all the black straight lines inside each umbrella. Cut each umbrella into halves along the red dotted lines. Each half makes one stellation. Don't cut the internal 5 triangles apart, and don't cut the curved sky blue lines: Their arrows show the territory of each unit.

These templates' size corresponds to the small dodecahedron net on p. 20. Use that net as a guide for laying out the stellated dodecahedron.

1 Small stellated dodecahedron

2 Small stellated dodecahedron

3 Small stellated dodecahedron

4 Small stellated dodecahedron

5 Small stellated dodecahedron

6 Small stellated dodecahedron

7 Small stellated dodecahedron

8 Small stellated dodecahedron

9 Small stellated dodecahedron

This green box isn't a template, it's a size check. To ensure that pieces are the correct size on your printouts, this box should measure 1.5" x 1.5". If not, check printout settings and adjust to "Print actual size".

Large Stellated Dodecahedron Templates

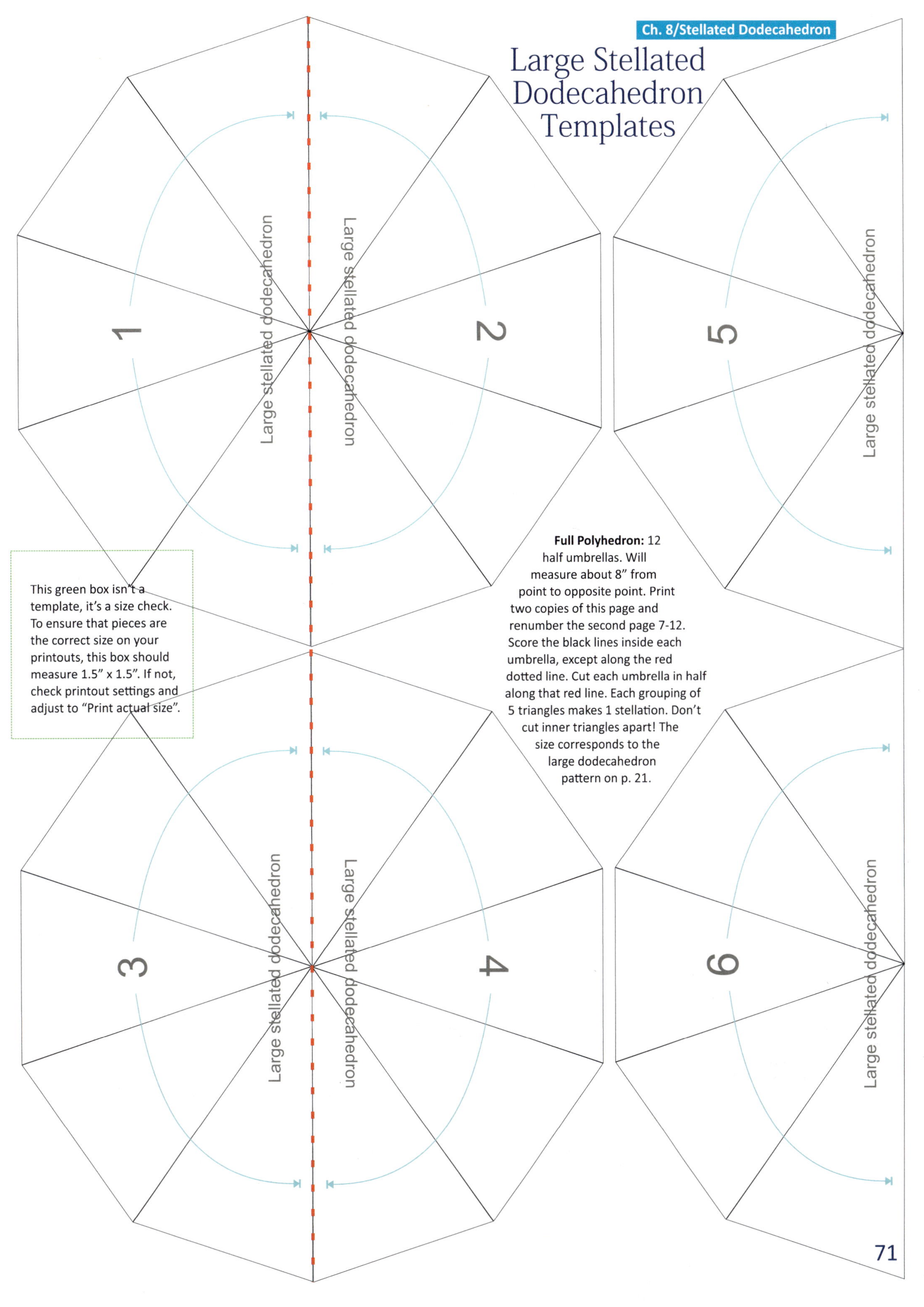

This green box isn't a template, it's a size check. To ensure that pieces are the correct size on your printouts, this box should measure 1.5" x 1.5". If not, check printout settings and adjust to "Print actual size".

Full Polyhedron: 12 half umbrellas. Will measure about 8" from point to opposite point. Print two copies of this page and renumber the second page 7-12. Score the black lines inside each umbrella, except along the red dotted line. Cut each umbrella in half along that red line. Each grouping of 5 triangles makes 1 stellation. Don't cut inner triangles apart! The size corresponds to the large dodecahedron pattern on p. 21.

Index

Want to Explore More?

Want more polyhedra? More challenge? Not sure what you want? Here are places to go for inspiration.

1. Wikipedia is loaded with polyhedra. Each entry will lead you to more, and there are nets for many of them. Start with the entry for "polyhedron" and follow the links from there!

2. "Paper Models of Polyhedra" https://www.polyhedra.net/en/. Gijs Korthals Altes' fantastic site. Dozens of polyhedron nets to download, print out and make from paper (which you can adopt to fabric with techniques in this book).

3. Stella Polyhedron Navigator
https://www.software3d.com/Stella.php. Robert Webb's programs let you view and even invent polyhedra. There are four levels: *Small Stella* has 300 nets, *Great Stella* has more, plus tools for creating trillions of polyhedra! The higher-level programs bring polyhedra into the 4th dimension, show cross sections, and other amazing stuff. All are modestly priced. If you're overwhelmed by the complexity, simply buy their merchandise – especially the calendar with luscious models of mind-blowing, intricate, weird and wonderful polyhedra!

Questions? Comments? Photos?

Share your thoughts! I would love to hear from you and see photos of your work! Email me at cathy.perlmutter@gmail.com

Follow me on social media:
Instagram: @cathyperlmutter
Facebook: https://www.facebook.com/cathy.perlmutter
Blog: http://www.gefiltequilt.com

I teach classes and do presentations for quilt and sewing guilds. See more of my quilts and 3D work on my website, at cathyperlmutter.com.

Most of my patterns and books are available from my etsy shop, at https//www.etsy.com/shop/CathyPStudio.

Made in United States
Cleveland, OH
28 June 2025

18062758R10045